Soulful Living

How to Live a More Conscious Life

Claus Böckmann

© Claus Böckmann 2012

All rights reserved

No part of this publication may be reproduced, stored in a retrieval system, or transmitted in any form or by any means, without the prior permission in writing of the publisher, nor be otherwise circulated in any form of binding or cover other than that in which it is published and without a similar condition including this condition being imposed on the subsequent purchaser.

First published in Great Britain by Pen Press

All paper used in the printing of this book has been made from wood grown in managed, sustainable forests.

ISBN 978-1-78003-308-2

Printed and bound in the UK
Pen Press is an imprint of
Indepenpress Publishing Limited
25 Eastern Place
Brighton
BN2 1GJ

A catalogue record of this book is available from the British Library

Cover design Jacqueline Abromeit

My sincere thanks for the thorough editing of Cindy Lee. Her editing has truly enriched this book.

About the Author

Claus Böckmann worked as an NLP master practitioner, a hypnotherapist and a healer for many years. In this capacity, he worked with people and their conscious/unconscious minds, helping them to heal themselves by finding a more positive perspective. He has also worked in IT and sales for more than a decade.

Drawing inspiration from his own experiences and from his observation of life, Claus brings a unique perspective to the issues of soulful living. During his lifetime, Claus has successfully recovered from near-bankruptcy several times, has changed both his country and profession, and has faced considerable private and professional pressures. All of these experiences have enabled him to develop a perspective of soul, kindness and compassion, and an increasing ability to let go of fear in life.

From his long personal experience, Claus knows about the fear that arises if we solely identify with our body, mind or emotions. *Soulful Living* offers an inspiring perspective of living from the centre of who we are, together with all we have become in our life. The book explores and describes whom we might want to see ourselves as and how we can live a more soulful life. Many examples drawn from real life will inspire the reader. Reading this book will help the reader to find a soulful perspective for themselves.

Claus is available for public speaking, consultancy/training and teaching, therapy and healing. Further information and descriptions of Claus's other books, *Success – A Different Measure* (Raider Publishing, 2011) and *A Loving Company* (Pen Press, 2011) can be found at *www.clausbockmannbooks.org*.

Contents

Introduction — 1

Three Approaches to Life — 4

The Dance of Life – Who Are We? — 10
The Psyche and the Mind — 11
    The Psyche
    The Conscious Mind
    The Subconscious Mind
    The Unconscious Mind
    Higher Consciousness
The Personality and the Ego — 14
    The Personality
    The Ego
The Spirit and the Soul — 21
    The Spirit
    The Soul
    Traditional Views
    The Present
    Soul Awareness
    Living from Soul
The Body — 29
Who We Are Not — 33
A Few Words About Language — 34
The Game of Life — 38
    Subjective Reality: How Do We Relate to Life?
    The Nature of the Game
    The Purpose of the Game
    Playing the Game
    Playing at the Higher Level
    Breaking Open
    Learning from the Game
    Soul Reality
    'Mistakes'
    Oneness

Creativity
Who Owns Our Happiness?
Duality
Soul Skill Living
Loving Our Bodies
Service
The Nature of the Rules
We Are the Game
Why Do We Play?
The Maestro
We Are All of This   61

Soulful Living   **65**
A Loving Life or a Life Driven by the Ego-Mind?   65
Daily Life   68
Listen   70
    Ericka
Go with the Flow of Life   76
Balance   78
    David
A Step at a Time   84
    Jane

Soulful Living and Nature   **88**
Rain   88
The Wind and Cold   90

Soulful Living in the Practice of Life I   **93**
Ask Your Soul for Guidance   93
Stay Open to Life   96
    Frank
Slowing Down and Resting   101
Eating, Drinking and Resting   103
    Overeating

Soulful Living and Spiritual Discipline — 106
Spiritual Discipline — 106
- Intention
- Attention

Soulful Living and Healing — 113
Healing Our Physical Body — 113
Healing Our Emotions — 115
- Tears and Sadness
- Peter
- Transforming Emotions

Healing Our Mind — 120
Soul Communication – Healing and Health — 128
- Mind-Body-Emotion
- Martha
- Disease
- Music Is a Great Healer

Soulful Living in the Practice of Life II — 140
Our Past Does Not Define Us — 140
Past Present Future — 142
Our Internal and External Worlds — 147
- John

The Power of Difficult Choices — 151
Right Time, Right Age? — 155
What Am I Entitled To? — 157
Awareness of Life — 161
Our Impact on Others — 164
Are We There Yet? — 167

Soulful Living and Life as the Impetus for Change — 171
Maurice and Roger — 171
In the World but Not Of It — 173
Acceptance of Life — 179
- Judy

James
Trust and Patience
Kim
Feeling Helpless
Barbara

Soulful Living and Love — 199
Unconditional Love — 199
Love for Ourselves and Love for Others — 201
    Pleasing Others
Unconditional Love – The Foundation of Life — 207
Looking for Love Outside Ourselves — 210
    Peggy and Tom
Love and Sexuality — 217
Love and Emotion — 220
Love and Friendship — 223
Soul Mates — 225
Spiritual Love — 227
Love in the World — 229

Soulful Living and Raising Our Children — 231
Physical Nurturing — 233
Emotional Nurturing — 235
Spiritual Nurturing — 236
Role Models — 238
Discipline — 242
Communication — 243
More on the Natural Spirituality of Children — 244
The Value of Time Spent in Nature — 248
Valuing Our Children's Thoughts — 249
Valuing Our Children's Imagination — 251
Valuing Our Children's Dreams — 252
Love Is Always Stronger than Fear — 255
    Mark

To Recap: A Few Reminders With Which to Close **260**
Soul and Ego in the Game of Life 260
The Getting of Wisdom 261
The Liberation of Learning that We Are Not Our Emotions 263
Intention and Service 265

Introduction

Most of us lead hectic lives, focussed on the daily routine of income, bills, schools etc. and distracted by concerns – about such personal fears as a lack of money, or about growing old and frail, and wider concerns about the state and safety of the wider world in which we live and which we will leave for our children; there are too many examples of natural disasters, political unrest, war, and the ever-present threat/reality of climate change.

In our daily lives, we rush from the early morning school run to the workplace, spend our working days trying to meet tight schedules and then dash to pick up our children at the day's end, often battling through traffic on the way home. Once there, we throw together a family supper (or reheat a supermarket-bought ready-made one), put the children to bed and then collapse in front of the TV for a little while before falling exhaustedly into bed ourselves, ready to repeat the routine in all too few hours' time.

Our minds and bodies constantly race to catch up with each other. When we are at work we worry about home. When we come home, we bring our work anxieties (and sometimes even our work itself if deadlines are looming) home with us. We seem to exist in a perpetual cycle of activity and anxiety, rather like the hamster in his cage: constantly running, never stopping and never arriving. At least a hamster is lucky enough to have a caring owner and will receive regular supplies of food and fresh bedding. Alas, in our case, we must provide good care for ourselves, and so often we do not.

To live in such a state is to live from a perspective of fear, in which we live within, operate from and are determined by only the shallow, external attributes of our lives – the aspects of who we appear to be. Such aspects include our genes, our gender, our race, our nationality, our culture, our language, our personality, our ego, our sexual orientation, our heritage, our social class, our wealth or lack of it and our occupation or lack of it, to name just a few!

The purpose of this book is to remind us that it is possible to live from a different perspective and to operate from a deeper level of being: a perspective of love and a soul-level of being. When we live from that level, our expression of who we are in our daily lives – as individuals, lovers, parents, children, siblings, co-workers etc. – becomes informed with love, compassion, wisdom, patience, trust and peace.

When we operate from a soulful, loving perspective, we are fully engaged in life. We become more fully aware, more fully alive, and all of our external attributes cease to rule us, simply becoming tools through which we learn about and express our higher nature.

This book will show how we can transform our lives in the process of discovering ourselves. It will explore how we can imbue our existence with a soulful energy and insight that will transform our lives from within. Many examples of issues in practical life, together with little stories about people, will help the reader to draw inspiration for themselves.

It is not a work that offers an instantly efficacious and effortless universal panacea. Beginning to live more consciously from soul does not mean that our lives will become pure laughter and sunshine, and that all difficulties will cease. When we see ourselves from a perspective of who we are more deeply, however, we begin to strengthen and increase the tools that we have to cope with life. With growing awareness comes an ability to shift our perspective more and more quickly to one of calmness, objectivity, compassion, peace, joy, patience and trust. We become wiser, more imaginative, more insightful and more intuitive. Problems start to find solutions more easily. Our confusion lessens. We become more resilient in the face of stressful situations, and when experiencing disasters beyond our control.

In essence, we come to live in a more loving, meaningful and useful way. We come to live a soulful life.

Three Approaches to Life

Paulina is a very bright, no-nonsense, highly intellectual Philosophy graduate. She has a fondness for the works of Jean-Paul Sartre and is an instinctive existentialist. For her, life has a beginning and an end, and we must all try to do our best in between. For Paulina, there is no transcendent force, no God, no source, and all notions of religion, and even of spirituality, are laughable mumbo-jumbo. All the decisions of her life are based on sound reasoning and taking personal responsibility. Given a world that she cannot change, she reacts to it as logically and as best she can. She often complains about the burden of life, and of being alone, but Paulina uses her fine intellectual mind to reason away all such existential angst.

At the same time, however, Paulina is a woman who expresses qualities which many observers would describe as being clearly 'soulful'. She is very loyal to her friends, deeply compassionate, empathetic, non-judgmental and an excellent listener. She values patience, trust, kindness and perseverance, and embodies these qualities in herself. She does not crave excitement or distraction, and has discovered that through quiet contemplation she can find a deep, restful stillness within herself. Paulina eschews the word 'soulful' on principle, and describes the qualities she values and possesses as being 'humane'. She also feels passionately that every member of the human race should come to consciously embody them; by so doing, they would change the world for the better.

Ruth is a spiritual healer, who participates in a number of local healing groups. She sees herself as a profoundly soulful person and believes that the fundamental purpose of her life is to be of service to others, to heal the sick and to comfort those in sorrow. Accordingly, she gives her time generously to each group, and to each patient, without any expectation of financial reward. She feels very strongly that the healing of her patients, and their gratitude, is payment enough.

Ruth also, however, has another quality to her healing persona: a considerable competitive streak. She loves to discuss who is the most passionate and effective healer within a group, and will often comment on the healing powers of other group members in their absence. She assesses comparative healing strengths on the basis of comments by patients, and delights in mentioning that patients often feel a stronger healing force and a greater healing when in her own healing hands.

With the compassion and wisdom that comes from truly operating from a soulful, loving perspective, the other healers make no judgment of Ruth, allowing her to find her own limits and to make her own learning. They understand that her attitude and competitiveness come from fear and a lack of self-esteem.

Ruth's competitive streak is also expressed in a certain missionary zeal. She likes to use her knowledge and understanding of spiritual matters to educate her fellow healers and friends. She has explained to them many times, for example, that her spiritual heart centre radiates an intense divine love and that a Higher Source guides her every action. Ruth trusts completely in the Higher Source and connects to it daily through her meditation practice.

Ruth constantly looks for external confirmation of the agency of the Higher Source in her daily life. As an example of this, she habitually parks her car in a dark alley and 'makes it safe' by enclosing it in a bubble of divine light. She believes that, through this visualisation, the Higher Source will protect the car from thieves and vandals. On one recent occasion, the healing group members had occasion to see Ruth's learning and personal healing in action. She entered the healing room at the beginning of a session in a shocked and agitated state. Angrily, she explained to the other members that her car had been vandalised and the glove compartment ransacked. When the healers questioned what had happened, Ruth confessed that she had omitted to lock the car, but remained adamant that the vandalisation should not have happened, because she had invoked such a strong force of protection. She felt indignant and confused at being let down so badly by her Higher Source. The healers sat patiently while she calmed down, gently willing her to see the truth of the matter. Eventually, Ruth understood, and, smiling rather sheepishly, she said, 'I forgot to use my common sense first, didn't I? I won't forget to lock the car next time!'

John is a tall, good-looking, athletic and sociable high-achiever, whose professional expertise lies in marketing. He speaks fluent French, German and Spanish, and has already published a marketing-related book. John is a driven man. While director of marketing at a company for which he had worked for several years, he achieved the selling of his house and the purchase and moving into of a larger new house within the remarkably short timeframe of only six weeks.

Following his house move, John was suddenly made redundant from his job, but responded typically positively to this crisis by immediately setting himself up as a freelance marketing consultant. Within a very short period of time, he was working on substantial marketing projects for major companies and was able to demand a high daily fee for his services. He is currently engaged in overseeing international projects for several multi-national companies. Unsurprisingly, John is greatly respected by his friends and peers, many of whom are in awe, if not a little jealous, of his exceptionally high achievements in life.

John, however, does not regard himself as a success. In truth, he is spurred on by a constant fear of inadequacy and failure. He is convinced that he lacks the key abilities that would make him a truly effective marketing consultant, and spends his time being terrified that his inadequacies will be discovered. He compensates for his self-perceived weaknesses by working exceptionally long hours to make doubly sure that everything that he does is perfect. He worries constantly that he will not be able to find work in the future. Yes, his services are in great demand now, but he is convinced that this could change in an instant.

Whenever conversations with peers, friends or colleagues turn to spiritual – i.e. non-material or metaphysical – matters, John always appears to listen politely, but his eyes betray the fact that his mind is elsewhere on more practical matters. He is simply not interested in ideas that concern trust in life, in each other or in a force for good; nor is he interested in discussing how we might be able to create our lives in a co-creative process with that force and by supporting each other.

At the core of John's being is the sense that he does not belong, and so he cannot trust – in colleagues, in life, or even in himself. For John, life is about honing his small talents into skills and success through his own relentless hard work. Life is a competition, fraught with the risk and fear of failure, and he must be a lone wolf in order to succeed. In reality, and very sadly, because John feels himself to be so fundamentally 'not good enough', he ends up competing very largely with himself, rather than with other people.

*   *   *

Are there any commonalities in the different approaches to life described in these three stories?

Yes, in the sense that, no matter what our philosophy of life might be, we all have blind spots. To a greater or lesser degree, we focus on only a selected part of the landscape, a narrow vista, without seeing the whole vast and beautiful expanse laid out before us.

For so many of us, life is simply a physical journey from birth to death, in which we are born into a certain set of circumstances and throughout which we strive to achieve. Life is full of meetings and partings – parents, lovers, partners, children, colleagues, jobs and experiences. In this life-view, with luck, we acquire degrees of human love, of laughter, of a little wisdom, of pleasures and of material objects along the path of our inexorable progress towards death.

Might there, however, be a more conscious, more soulful, more powerful way of living, in which we are in contact with the deeper aspects of our being, beneath our individual circumstances, and in which we can become aware that we can co-create our lives and operate from a place of profound love, compassion, trust and peace? Our response to that question will determine our initial answer. As the stories of Paulina, Ruth and John show, the perspective that we take on life depends on who we think we are.

The Dance of Life – Who Are We?

'Who am I, and why am I here?'

If you are reading this book, the chances are that at some recent point in your life you have asked yourself those two fundamental questions and have not been quite satisfied with your answers. You might already be aware that you are not simply your personal background or biography; neither are you your nationality, or the religion that might have been given to you by your parents.

Perhaps you have found a degree of personal meaning by identifying yourself in terms of mythical or contemporary archetypes: for example, the sinner, the lone wolf, the earth mother, the alcoholic, the eco-warrior...

For some of you, there might already be a deeper sense of yourself as pure consciousness – of being consciousness experiencing itself. This might have come in the stillness and silence of a formal meditation practice, or in a sudden moment in nature, when your senses were awed by the beauty of a land or seascape and your mind was broken open by it. You might have been flooded with a sense of 'knowing', which came as a deep, quiet clarity and peace and a sensation of oneness with the universe around you, so profound and serene that all the language in your possession was too clumsy and inadequate to express it.

The Psyche and the Mind

The Psyche

The word 'psyche' comes from the original Greek *'psukhe'*, meaning 'breath, life, soul',[1] i.e. the breath of spirit, of life, which animates us. In our modern language, the meanings generally attributed to it are 'the human faculty for thought, judgment and emotion; the mental life, including both conscious and unconscious processes' and 'the vital mental or spiritual entity of the individual as opposed to the body'.[2] In essence, everything that we experience, and everything that we think or feel in response to our experiences, comes to each of us through our individual psyche. It is through our psyche that we apprehend the world without and within us, and through the psyche that we seek to understand it.

The Conscious Mind

The adjective 'conscious' comes from the Latin word *'conscius'*, meaning 'knowing with others or in oneself'. It is generally defined as 'having awareness of one's self, acts and surroundings',[3] or as 'that part of the psyche or mental functioning in which thoughts, ideas, emotions and other mental content are in complete awareness'.[4]

---

[1] *Oxford English Dictionary*, 2003
[2] *Mosby's Medical Dictionary*, 8th Ed., 2009
[3] *Dorland's Medical Dictionary for Health Consumers*, 2007
[4] *Mosby's Medical Dictionary*, 2009

The conscious mind works with the information that it receives from our senses, constantly collecting, interpreting and reacting to this data. It uses thought to work out how to do things. It makes decisions in the present moment, reviews the past in the form of memories, and makes projections into the future.

The Subconscious Mind

The word 'subconscious' refers to 'that part of the mind of which one is not fully aware, but which influences one's actions and feelings'.[5] The subconscious mind is that 'part of the mind below the level of conscious perception',[6] in which 'mental processes take place without the mind's being distinctly conscious of its own activity'.[7]

The subconscious mind works with symbols; it is the part of the mind that enables you to see a chair and know immediately, without thinking, that it is a chair. It is also the part of the mind that develops skills and both helpful and unhealthy habits; it is the subconscious, for example, that makes it difficult to give up an addiction such as smoking, even though our conscious mind knows that smoking can cause disease.

The conscious mind can only deal with a certain number of experiences. Our subconscious,

---

[5] *Oxford English Dictionary*, 2003
[6] *Mosby's Medical Dictionary*, 2009
[7] *Mosby's Dental Dictionary*, 2nd Ed., 2008

however, is vast and powerful. We react from it all the time without consciously realising it.

The Unconscious Mind

In psychoanalytic theory, the 'unconscious' is the area of the mind which contains 'elements of psychic makeup, such as memories or repressed desires, that are not subject to conscious perception or control, but that often affect conscious thoughts and behaviours'.[8]

In Jungian psychology, the 'collective unconscious' is deemed to be the part of the unconscious that is common to all mankind.

Higher Consciousness

You might also be aware of the term 'higher consciousness'. This term embodies the concept of an extraordinary state of consciousness.

In a non-spiritual sense, it can refer to a profound intellectual enlightenment and a mastery of one's mind. In a spiritual sense, however, it can refer to a transcendence of ordinary human consciousness, a visionary insight, the sense of oneness with the divine or creative force. There are many terms for 'higher consciousness', arising from many different spiritual traditions. These include, for example, 'supra', 'Buddhic' or 'Christ' consciousness.

---

[8] *The American Heritage Medical Dictionary*, 2004

The Personality and the Ego

The Personality

The personality can be described as the 'characteristics or qualities that form an individual's character'.[9] Our characteristics – i.e. the psychological features and idiosyncrasies that make each of us our own particular person – arise to some extent from our genes, and also from our responses to the environmental factors to which we are exposed.

Evidence suggests, for example, that levels of intelligence or neuroticism are inherited. Our social environment and the nature of our personal experiences, however, are crucial to the moulding of our personalities. As we develop through childhood and onwards, our personalities are influenced by many factors, including our parents, our peers, our culture, our education and the stratum of the socio-economic structure into which we have been born.

Our personalities influence, and are expressed in, the ways in which we think and behave. The ways in which we think and behave also affect our personalities – not least in the ways in which we deal with the consequences of our thoughts and actions. Our perceptions – our experience of our experiences – are filtered through our personality. If we think back to Paulina, Ruth and John, we can

---

[9] *Oxford English Dictionary*, 2003

see that our personalities determine the vista that we see, and indeed how we perceive it.

Although core traits will remain, our personalities evolve as we grow older in age and grow wider and deeper in experience and knowledge; our responses to the world become more complex, more fine-tuned and, with luck, more wise.

The Ego

'*Ego*' is the Latin word meaning 'I'. In the nineteenth century, it began to be used in English to denote the philosophical concept of the 'conscious self'. In the early part of the twentieth century, the psychologist Sigmund Freud included the concept of the ego as a key element in his psychoanalytic theory of how the mind works.

For Freud, the ego is 'that part of the mind that mediates between the conscious and the unconscious and is responsible for the interpretation of reality and the development of a sense of self'.[10] In Freudian theory, the ego regulates the instinctive impulses of the unconscious mind (termed the 'id'), such as aggression. The ego also creates and maintains defence mechanisms to protect the mind from emotional pain. Freud also posited the existence of a further component of the mind, the 'superego': a self-critical conscience formed between the ages of five and puberty, which uses absorbed social

---

[10] *Oxford English Dictionary*, 2003

standards to control the innate urges of the id through guilt.

Freudian psychoanalytic theory is one of the principal schools of modern psychodynamic therapy, which seeks to heal unhealthy aspects of a person's behaviour, for example addiction, by identifying and exploring factors in their unconscious mind, such as unresolved conflict, which find expression in their self-harming behaviour.

Derivatives of the word 'ego' include 'egoism', an eighteenth-century ethical theory that perceives self-interest to be the fundamental basis of morality, and 'egotism', a term also coined in the eighteenth century, which describes 'the quality of being excessively conceited or absorbed in oneself'.[11] In Freud's definition, 'ego' is a simple, neutral technical term describing a part of the mind's apparatus. In contemporary, everyday language, however, the word 'ego' has come to be commonly used, and understood, to mean 'a person's sense of self-esteem or self-importance'.[12]

All too often, that sense of self-esteem or self-importance can be perceived to be the key part of our personality – to be, indeed, who we are. How many of us, on a daily basis, are conscious of trying to balance our thoughts and feelings and actions, so that we avoid falling into the self-doubt

---

[11] *Oxford English Dictionary*, 2003
[12] *Ibid.*

and weakness of low self-esteem, or into the insensitivity and arrogance of conceit? To be accused of egotism, to be labelled 'egotistical', is a condemnation that most of us seek strongly to avoid.

Fundamentally, however, as Freud described, our ego is a valuable tool which helps us to be aware of the world, and to interact with and interpret it. To have a well-balanced, healthy ego is simply to have, and to operate from, a natural, realistic, peaceful consciousness of our worth and meaning in the world. A healthy ego means that our relationship to ourselves, to each other and to the world is also healthy. It enables compassion and empathy, and disables prejudice and bigotry.

When our ego is in equilibrium, when there is neither subservience nor dominance in our response to the world around us, but only a clear, cool, objective awareness, we can begin to perceive that we are operating from a different level of consciousness, a higher level, a 'soul-level', which senses and understands that we are all equal. At this level, we cease to operate from ego, but without any need to condemn it. We understand that our egos are not inherently bad, negative or dangerous, and that, in fact, having a healthy, balanced ego is vital to our human development and wellbeing.

When we are children, our egos begin to form as we develop language, and as we become aware of and interact with the world around us. The ego plays its part in teaching us many lessons. It helps us to balance our instinctive desires against the demands of our physical and social reality. It helps us to understand how to behave appropriately in the world. It keeps us safe. When we have yet to understand this, however, it is all too easy for us to operate from ego in an unbalanced, unhealthy way. When we see ourselves as different to others, as better or worse, worth less or worth more, as superior or inferior, we operate from imbalance, from a place of misperception.

The ego is concerned very largely with the material, physical world and our place in it. The messages of competition and success that we receive through our education and culture (and even from our primal sexual and aggressive drives) lead many, if not most, of us to believe that material success – the extent to which we possess (or do not) wealth, beauty, power, influence – determines our worth. This belief, and the extent to which we 'succeed' or 'fail' by its definition, can cause great damage, resulting in the equal illusions of self-aggrandisement or self-abasement. Most importantly, it blocks our 'soul-level' sense of who we really are.

The soul-level sense understands that, in essence, we are the totality of our being. We are not simply our bodies, nor our minds, nor that part of our mind that is our ego, nor our catalogue of personal successes and failures. When we experience soul-level understanding, we come to begin to know the 'divine' aspect of ourselves. 'Divine' means 'of, or like, a God or god'[13] and is, undoubtedly, a word that evokes powerful responses, both positive and negative.

It is the purpose of this book, however, to show you that however you define yourself – as a devout atheist convinced that 'spirituality' is a delusion; as a devout practitioner of a recognised religion; as an agnostic; as a person who is 'spiritual but not religious'; as a person who feels that they are 'a divine being on a human journey' – it does not matter, because the experience of your 'divine' self, and the wonder of living from that self, is entirely possible for all of us.

So, what is that 'divine self'? It is the deepest part of us – the consciousness that is conscious of itself. It is the place of awe and wonder in which we know that we are expressions of the creative force that animates the universe and everything in it. It is 'divine' because it itself both emanates from and is that creative force. It is the self that knows that there is no separation between each of us, between us and every other living thing, between us and everything in the incredibly beautiful physical world and universe in which we live.

Language can sometimes be a clumsy tool. Trying to describe the sensation of experiencing the divine self, trying to describe the profound love and joy and clarity and compassion that comes from that experience, is like trying to contain the Pacific

---

[13] *Oxford English Dictionary*, 2003

Ocean within a puddle. Language is inadequate for the task, but, in truth, the experience does not need language – it speaks for itself, wordlessly.

This is a book, however, which must use words to convey its meaning, however clumsy they might be. Apart from deliberations as to who we are or not, it is the examples of practical life, spiritual discipline, healing, bringing up our children, love and service and how we respond to or initiate it that will show us if and how we can live from a soulful perspective, the perspective of us as a divine self.

Suffice to say, then, that when we let go of operating from our ego, and when we begin to see and feel and experience ourselves beyond it – when we go deeper and begin to feel ourselves on the soul-level – we begin to experience a different level of perception. We begin to experience that sense of ourselves as pure, loving consciousness, as an expression of creation – as both the drop of water and the vast ocean of which that drop is a tiny part. We cease to feel difference and separation. There is a profound sense of peace and harmony, a beautiful, joyful, quiet, loving clarity and compassion. At the moment that we feel this love and peace within ourselves, we come to know that we are not simply our egos. In this place of soul, there is no discontent. There is only love. When we let go of operating from our egos, we still have our bodies and our minds and our egos, but we are not ruled by them – they are only a part of who we are – and we begin to operate from the deepest, timeless place of wisdom and love: the divine soul self.

The Spirit and the Soul

Many scholarly, religious and metaphysical works have been written over the centuries discussing the nature of reality, the existence of God, the nature of God (if God exists), the nature of what it is to be human, the nature of consciousness, the mind's relationship to the body, the existence of the soul, the nature of the soul, the existence of the spirit, the nature of the spirit, the relationship of soul and spirit to the mind, etc., etc...

Different religions, philosophical schools and cultures have subtly differing definitions of terms such as 'divine', 'God', 'soul' and 'spirit'. The concepts to which these terms refer are also subject to the shift and evolution of thought and understanding over time within the individual religions, philosophies and cultures themselves.

You, too, will have come to this book with your own definitions of 'spirit' and 'soul'. They might be very clear, informed, perhaps, by a formal religious education. Equally, your definitions might be slightly muddy and inchoate, formed from half-remembered childhood lessons mixed with ideas gleaned from contemporary texts on spirituality and self-help.

Here below you will find offered definitions of 'spirit' and 'soul'. It is important to state, though, that, whatever your response might be to them, your own instinctive understanding of 'spirit' and 'soul', your own sense of your own soulful life and your experience of living it are, and always will be, uniquely yours, evolving, growing and deepening over time just as you yourself grow in experience and wisdom.

The Spirit

The noun 'spirit' comes from the Latin words '*spiritus*', meaning 'breath, spirit', and '*spirare*', meaning 'breathe'. In common language, 'spirit' tends to be defined variously as: 'the non-physical part of a person, which is the seat of emotions and character; the soul; such a part regarded as a person's true self and as capable of surviving physical death or separation; such a part manifested as an apparition after death; a ghost; a supernatural being'.[14]

'Spirit' can also be defined as 'an animating or vital principle held to give life to physical organisms'[+]. In this sense, it is a non-quantifiable energy that infuses all living things. The adjective 'spiritual' and the further noun 'spirituality' also derive from the same Latin roots. 'Spiritual' is commonly defined as 'that which relates to or affects the human spirit or soul as opposed to material or physical things'.[15] 'Spirituality' is defined as 'the state, quality, manner or fact of being spiritual'.[16]

---

[14] *Oxford English Dictionary*, 2003
[15] *Ibid.*
[16] *Ibid.*

When we talk about the spiritual aspects of life, we normally think about our higher nature, our better choices in life, and the creative qualities that we express.

The Soul

The noun 'soul' comes from the Old English word '*sawol*', which in turn comes from the early Germanic word '*saiwala*'. Each has a similar meaning: the principle of life in man or animals. From circa 971, '*sawol*' also came to mean the spirit of someone who has died. This might be because it is related to another early Germanic word '*saiwaz*', meaning 'sea', and in the religious mythology of the time it might have been thought that the souls of the dead took rest at the bottom of the sea.

'Soul' can be defined as: '1. the principle of life, feeling, thought and action in humans, regarded as a distinct entity separate from the body, and commonly held to be separable in existence from the body; the spiritual part of humans as distinct from the physical part; 2. the spiritual part of humans regarded in its moral aspect, or as believed to survive death and be subject to happiness or misery in a life to come; 3. the disembodied spirit of a deceased person'.[++]

Traditional Views

In western religious, metaphysical and cultural traditions, our understanding of 'spirit' and 'soul' is heavily influenced by the Christian Bible and by Catholicism. In the western Catholic tradition, the term 'spirit' invokes the Holy Spirit, which together with God the Father and God the Son (Jesus Christ) comprises the Holy Trinity. The Holy Spirit is no less than God immanent within us.

In this tradition, the 'soul' is seen as the conscious, responsible part of us that will pass from life at death to reside in Purgatory, Heaven or Hell depending on the goodness of our behaviour and actions during life. Culturally, the 'soul' can be used as a synonym for a person's moral nature. Although 'spirit' can be synonymous with 'ghost', 'lost souls' too are sometimes believed to wander the earth until they find peace.

In eastern religious, metaphysical and cultural traditions, such as Hinduism, individual souls reincarnate: are born, live and die in successive bodies, again and again. They are incarnated within each new life to learn the lessons to be derived from that life, and each new life is an opportunity to move nearer to wisdom and enlightenment. During each life, each soul incurs debts, or 'karma', and, when reborn, it is reborn into a life that reflects that karma.

It is interesting to note that the Nag Hammadi library, a collection of more than 50 early Christian texts discovered in Upper Egypt in 1945, revealed that early Christian mystics, known as the Christian Gnostics, also preached a doctrine of reincarnation, later judged by the Church to be heretical. Gnostic texts discovered at Nag Hammadi include the Gospel of Thomas, the Gospel of Philip and the Gospel of Truth. These gospels are excluded from the official Biblical canon.

Finally, in some western and eastern 'animist' traditions, such as eastern Shinto and western Paganism, plants, inanimate objects and natural phenomena such as the wind are also believed to be infused with spirit or to have souls.

The Present

In contemporary times, a natural evolution in spiritual awareness and understanding is occurring, whereby many spiritual practitioners are moving away from fixed traditional religious and metaphysical concepts and are developing a new form of spirituality.

This form, of which this book is a humble example, expresses a synthesis of certain elements of western and eastern concepts of spirit and soul, together with, *inter alia*, elements of psychology, quantum physics and the concept of mind-body-spirit ('holistic') health. Through this synthesis comes a deeper, more autonomous and empowering understanding of our experience of being, expressing and delighting in the divine life force that animates us.

As indicated above, the terms 'spirit' and 'soul' are often used interchangeably, but, although they are closely connected, there are subtle differences. For those readers who appreciate simple signposts by which to navigate the landscape in which they find themselves, 'spirit' here is taken to mean the 'divinity', or creative life force, which infuses and animates each one of us and which is present throughout the universe, and 'soul' is the individuated aspect of that divinity that we each are but of which we might not automatically be aware.

Soul Awareness

The soul can be seen as the self-aware essence unique to a particular living being. It, rather than the brain or any other material part of the biological organism, is the true essence of each being. The soul can be defined as the internal principle, beyond and beneath ego and mind (the 'ego-mind'), by which we think, feel and will. To use a very simple analogy: if our soul is the driver, our body is the vehicle in which and through which our soul navigates and experiences the material world.

The soul expresses itself through the will, which can be defined as 'the faculty by which a person decides on and initiates action'.[17] We are what we will. We cannot refuse to will, as that refusal is in itself a willing. On a day-to-day basis, it is in the decisions taken by our will that we come closest to experiencing our soul. When our will chooses actions that are loving, health-giving and of service to others, for example, it is operating from the soul.

---

[17] *Oxford English Dictionary*, 2003

When, however, it chooses actions that are fearful, harmful to others (or to ourselves) or selfish, it is operating at a more superficial level than the soul; it is operating from the ego-mind. It is, indeed, through awareness of the choices of the will that we grow towards understanding, and living from, our soul.

We are drawn to the concept of soul because of the mystery of life and death and consciousness – of what it is to be 'human', to be *homo sapiens sapiens*. Notwithstanding its accuracy on the biological level, evolutionary theory cannot fully account for the profound sense of soul recognition that many of us experience. When people say that they have lost their soul, they mean that, through the pain of extreme fear, they have come to feel that they have lost the truest, deepest part of themselves.

Some people regard their soul as a part of themselves, whereas others feel that their soul is a separate entity to which they are attached. These ideas, however, are only mind constructs, which can actually serve to distance us from the quiet, wordless experience of soul. In truth, it is enough simply to acknowledge the deeper soul aspect of ourselves, without striving to know exact details; one does not need to dismantle the wings of a dragonfly to comprehend the beauty of its delicate flight.

We might each not automatically be aware of our soul, but a soul can become aware of itself, and be aware that it is distinct from the personality and the ego-mind that is connected to it. This awareness is a part of what is called 'spiritual enlightenment'. 'Enlightenment' also embodies the immanent understanding of the oneness of all things.

Living from Soul

Spirit and soul are aspects of the coherent whole that comprises each of us as human beings, and which includes our ego-mind, personality and body, our thoughts and emotions, and our lives. Each aspect is an element of the whole of us, and each aspect must be healthy and in balance, both within itself and with every other aspect, if we are to live healthily and coherently and with awareness – if we are to live a soulful, conscious life.

Essential to a coherent way of living, for example, is an awareness of our perspective in any moment: an awareness of from which part of our whole being a decision is being made. The key question that we come to ask ourselves is: are we operating from the narrow, superficial view of the ego-mind, or from the deeper, wider understanding of soul?

Once we begin to become aware of ourselves at the soul level, we naturally begin to live a more loving, generous, compassionate, self-responsible and empowered life. In an interesting echo of Paulina's humane existentialism, once we begin to live from the perspective of our own soul, we cease to give responsibility for our behaviour and wellbeing to a higher authority, but take responsibility for ourselves. We come to live truly authentically.

As long as we are unaware of our soul, or we simply deny the possibility of its existence, our ego-mind will govern our outer and inner life, and we might chose to abdicate responsibility for ourselves to our concept of God or Fate. Once we are aware of our soul, however, and chose to operate from it, we become clear and empowered, and our ego-mind assumes the healthy role of an excellent and efficient tool: a tool which our soul can use to express itself.

Our spirit, soul, mind and body give full expression to who we are. When our thoughts and actions are governed from our divine, soul-level perspective, our deepest self occupies the driving seat and our ego-mind is a helpful passenger. The ego-mind continually has to work out its responses to life, based on its store of education (or the lack of it), experience and conditioning. Our divine, creative soul aspect, however, will always have a different perspective from our ego-mind, because it will always make choices out of love. It will never make choices out of fear. The soul choice is always for love.

The Body

Our souls evolve in wisdom as they learn through the medium of our minds and bodies. Just as much as our ego-minds and personalities, our bodies are vital tools for the learning of our souls.

Everything that we are – spirit, soul, ego-mind, thoughts, emotions and personality – is expressed via our physical body. Our bodies have their own intelligence. Our brains, through a beautifully complex biofeedback system of synaptic connections and chemical signals, regulate their functions without conscious intervention on our part. Just think, for one moment, of the fact that when we are in deep unconscious sleep our lungs still breathe, our hearts still pump, our skin and capillaries still effectively regulate our body temperature.

Our bodies are living, self-regulating organisms, highly sensitive to, and highly attuned to, their external and internal environments. As such, as much as they can relax and reinvigorate in the warmth of the sun, or be bruised and broken by blunt force, they are also deeply affected by our ego-mind's internal state of wellbeing or dis-ease. Our bodies are excellent, subtle barometers of our emotional and mental states. It is highly likely that all of us, at some time, will have made the painful discovery of shoulders knocking against ears through locked-in anxiety, or have felt our spines click into misalignment as their supporting muscles turn bullet-hard and spasm through accreted, unacknowledged tension. Science, too, acknowledges that psychological stress detrimentally affects our immune systems.

Soulful living means honouring our body: by eating healthily, resting well and paying attention to the messages that our body gives to us, both of pleasure and of discomfort. Any discomfort is a message telling us that we are not paying sufficient attention in our lives: that we are not living from soul. The message of illness might be, for example, that we are working too hard, or that we are refusing to acknowledge that we are trapped in a job or relationship that is preventing us from fulfilling who we are – from being who our soul knows us to be.

It might be that we are also paying too much attention to, and absorbing too much of, the stresses of the world. Yes, we need to be aware of what is happening in the world, and, yes, we all have a vital role in ensuring that we bring only love, compassion and generosity of spirit to all of our dealings with the world. It is all too easy, however, for us to become over-exposed to negative influences within our external environment. How often, for example, are violence and horror elements of the films or television programmes that we choose to watch, or of the books that we choose to read, or of the music to which we choose to listen? Equally, how many of us feel overwhelmed by all the trouble and death in the world, which pours into our homes and minds via the reports that we read and see from across the world's media?

Our body is a perfect tool of expression; its awareness helps us to regulate and change our responses to those areas of our lives that cause disease, so that we can arrive at a more soulful way of living: a way of living coherently, in which soul, ego-mind, personality and body are all in perfect balance. It is often said that disease is dis-ease left unattended, and, indeed, our bodies tend to scream louder and louder until we listen to them.

One of the most striking and wonderful results of beginning to live from the soul – of beginning to live from a deeper, more peaceful, joyful place of consciousness, awareness and clarity – is the ability to become increasingly aware of the effects of negative thought and emotion patterns on our bodies. There are many excellent texts on this subject, including Louise L Hay's book *You Can Heal Your Life* (Hay House), now in its 20th Anniversary edition.

When our ego-mind is healthy, our physical body also tends to be healthy, and vice-versa. Each provides an invaluable feedback mechanism for the other. When we become conscious of the effects that our thoughts and emotions have on our body, we can begin to pay attention: to adjust, relax, breathe, meditate, and thereby release the dis-ease within our body. In so doing, not only do we help our bodies to be healthy, but we also raise our consciousness to operate from our soul level. As we do so again and again, we begin to come to a natural place where we live from the soul, and not from the ego-mind. Soul, ego-mind and body begin to work in perfect, coherent, balanced harmony. The proof of this is that, at every level, we begin to make choices from love, rather than from fear.

Who We Are Not

In some ways, it is easier to understand who we are by understanding what it is that we are not. To recap, we are neither the vehicle nor the instruments that we use to navigate the world.

We are not our physical self, although our physical self is a tool for expressing who we are. We are not the body that is born, that moves through space and time, and that eventually dies. We are not what we eat or drink, although what we eat and drink shows us a good deal about whether or not our relationship to our body is a loving, healthy one.

We are not our sexual self, nor are we our emotional self, and we are not the unique bundle of idiosyncrasies and neuroses that might occupy and find expression through our ego-mind. We are neither our intelligence nor our rational mind. We are not our personality, nor are we its components; we are not our gender, our race, our nationality, our culture, our family, our job, our personal history nor our genetic blueprint.

We are neither our place nor our function in society. We are neither the damaged victim of a dysfunctional family, nor a superior being because we have been born into ease and privilege. The ego-mind may lament and resent and choose to be victimised by the shortcomings and short-change of an imperfect body, or of a poverty-stricken or difficult childhood, or of a heartbroken or overlooked adulthood, but that is not who we are.

We are, rather, our 'divine' self: the soul that sits calmly at the heart of all of these external attributes. We are the clear, quiet energy that operates always from love. We are the wisdom gained from our navigations through the world; the wisdom that finds, learns and expresses love no matter if the straights through which we navigate are serene or storm-tossed. We are the soul that chooses love, because it is love.

A Few Words About Language

Language is a vital tool both for understanding the world around us and for expressing ourselves within it. As conscious human beings, we have the delight of being able to communicate who we are through a multiplicity of languages. There is the language of our bodies: our gestures, postures, actions, facial expressions, our tears, and the look of love, fear or anger in our eyes. Some of the most powerful ways in which we connect with each other, recognise each other and share our experience as human beings come through the wordless languages of the music that we compose, the dance that we choreograph, the art that we create.

Equally, the abstract language of mathematics, of real and imaginary numbers, of beautiful Fibonacci sequences and fractals, of relativity formulae and quantum theory, is helping us to arrive at increasingly accurate scientific explanations of the workings of the complex universe and world in which we exist. The language of words – what we say and write, and how we say and write it, and the language of words that our minds use to express how we think and feel – is fundamentally important to our relationship to both the world within us and the world without us.

As children, through spoken language, we begin to establish the ego (the 'me' centre) and to communicate with the other (the world beyond the 'me'). We use language to describe, learn about and assimilate our internal and external experience. As our language of words develops, however, we can be swallowed by the 'reality' that it creates. Through words we conceptualise both the world around us and our experience of it. We use our concepts to order the world and to place ourselves within it, and to express our present experience, to recall the past and to posit the future.

Concepts mediate our experience of the world; through them we assign meaning to objects, events and experiences. Essentially, our concepts are stories, and the stories that our minds choose to create are formed from the synthesis of the information received through our direct experience, through our own unique mental and emotional landscape, and through the habitual ways of thinking which we have derived and developed from, *inter alia*, our education, our culture, our families, our religion, our politics, our own experience.

If we live from soul, we develop the ability to maintain and apply an alert awareness and objective clarity to all our concepts. We cease to absorb and parrot received concepts, for example, but examine these through the filter of our own growing experience and the wisdom that grows with that experience. We keep our concepts sharp and fresh and constantly adaptable.

A classic example of a culturally received concept that many of us adopt without question can be found in contemplating the idea of a perfect garden. The accepted norm is that the deliberately planted flowers in the garden are beautiful, whereas the natural plants that have found their own way into the garden are ugly 'weeds' that must be eradicated before they take over. Next time you stand in a garden, look without prejudice at the hand-cultivated fragile roses and at the irrepressibly energetic bindweed with its heart-shaped leaves and bell-like flowers and decide upon, feel into your own instinctive sense of their relative beauty. Is one truly more beautiful than the other – more worthy of its place in the garden than the other? Now apply this objective clarity to every concept that you possess, and you will glimpse the freedom of intelligence that we experience when we begin to live from soul.

Our minds' ability to use the language of words to conceptualise our internal and external worlds, and to share ourselves with each other, is a marvellous aspect of our existence as conscious human beings. The more highly developed our language of words, the better able we become to express ourselves accurately. The development of a supple, extensive, multi-faceted vocabulary is indeed crucial to our mental and emotional wellbeing. If we possess such a vocabulary there is (almost) nothing that we might think or feel that we are not able to express. If, however, we lack the vocabulary to either understand or accurately express a thought or feeling, its expression must find a voice in other languages. All too often, for example, fear and its concomitants – hurt, pain and anger – come to be expressed in the language of physical violence to others and/or to ourselves.

All languages convey meaning, and that meaning has an energy to which we respond with our emotions and thoughts. We can feel uplifted, for example, by the relationship of notes in an overture, the rhythm of bodies moving in perfect harmony, the sequence of syllables in a stanza, the resonance between human hand and the perfection of nature in the curve of a polished stone set against a landscape, the spell-binding power of a master orator. We can also feel assaulted by language that has been deliberately chosen for its angry, ugly vulgarity. We can be disheartened, made hopeless, by language that is itself an expression of dis-ease and an over-focus on the negative.

When we come to live from soul, we learn to choose our language carefully. We learn to carefully choose what we express. We learn to use, and then come naturally to choose, language that conveys the energy of love, joy, positivity and peace: language that, for example, expresses every 'problem' as an opportunity for love, learning and growth. When we live from soul, however, we also come to know that there are some states of being that language cannot adequately express: states for which language is inadequate, for which concepts are more like straitjackets, because they are too small to contain the meaning, the energy, of those states. When we experience oneness, when we experience our soul, when we live from our divine selves, we come to know that which Lao Tzu describes in chapter one of the *Tao Te Ching*: 'The nameless is the beginning of heaven and earth'.

The Game of Life

Subjective Reality: How Do We Relate to Life?

The anthropologist, biologist, epistemologist and cyberneticist Gregory Bateson (1904–1980) was profoundly interested in the nature of the human mind: how we think, how we perceive reality, how ideas react and interact in our minds and, equally, how it is through nexuses of interacting ideas that we relate to each other and to the world outside ourselves.

Bateson was fascinated by and devoted much of his working life to the exploration of the meeting point, the point of communication, between our ideas and external reality. One of the central tenets of his work was that our perceptions of reality are subjective, are coloured by our ideas: we see what we expect to see, and we filter out what we don't. The ideas that we develop in response to reality allow us to navigate through the world, but they are not the world. It was also Bateson's view that the individual mind extended beyond the body through the communication of its ideas, and that, hence, it was a sub-system of a larger mind interconnected with society and with the physical world.

Dissatisfied with conventional theories of learning and evolution, Bateson sought to establish 'steps', or points of reference, to help map the nature of the interface between the mind and external reality. Further, he was fascinated by the patterns and rhythms of the process of ideation and interaction. He felt that through exploring the properties of these interactions it would be possible to come to a clearer understanding of the ways in which our minds connect with reality. This interaction and relationship between ideas Bateson called 'the ecology of mind'. He believed that the nature of human interactions such as play, for example, could be comprehended only within the context of an ecology of ideas.

Bateson also believed that creativity came from the serendipitous intermingling of different ideas. Furthermore, it was the point at which we began to sense that reality might not be what we perceived it to be that was revelatory, liberating, because it allowed creativity and exploration.

The Nature of the Game

Bateson developed a system of 'metalogues', derived from conversations with his daughter, to help both to express and to explore the nature of ideas and their relationship to reality. A metalogue is, in fact, a conversation in which both the content and the structure are used to explore and express a difficult subject. One of the most significant and difficult metalogues of all is that between man and nature. In the following metalogue, Bateson points to the ways in which we attempt to understand and to order the game of life – to make sense of our internal and external worlds – by seeking to grasp the nature of the 'rules' within which life, we perceive, requires us to live.

2.3 Metalogue: About Games and Being Serious

F: Let's go back to the question which you asked and which I said was too difficult to answer today. We were talking about the printer breaking up his clichés,[18] and you said that he would still keep some sort of order among his letters – to keep from going mad. And then you asked 'What sort of order should we cling to so that when we get into a muddle we do not go mad?' It seems to me that the 'rules' of the game is only another name for that sort of order.

---

[18] In printing, a cliché was a printing plate cast from movable type. This is also called a stereotype. When letters were set one at a time, it made sense to cast a phrase used repeatedly as a single slug of metal. (Source: Wikipedia)

D: Yes – and cheating is what gets us into muddles.

F: In a sense, yes. That's right. Except that the whole point of the game is that we do get into muddles, and do come out on the other side, and if there were no muddles our 'game' would be like canasta or chess – and that is not how we want it to be.

D: Is it *you* that make the rules, Daddy? Is that fair?

F: That, daughter, is a dirty crack. And probably an unfair one. But let me accept it at face value. Yes, it is I who make the rules – after all, I do not want us to go mad.

D: All right. But, Daddy, do you also change the rules? Sometimes?

F: Hmm, another dirty crack. Yes, daughter, I change them constantly. Not all of them, but some of them.

D: I wish you'd tell me when you're going to change them!

F: Hmm – yes – again. I wish I could. But it isn't like that. If it were like chess or canasta, I could tell you the rules, and we could, if we wanted to, stop playing and discuss the rules. And then we could start a new game with the new rules. But what rules would hold us between the two games? While we were discussing the rules?

D: I don't understand.

F: Yes. The point is that the purpose of these conversations is to discover the 'rules'. It's like life – a game whose purpose is to discover the rules, which rules are always changing and

      always undiscoverable.
D: But I don't call that a *game*, Daddy.
F: Perhaps not. I would call it a game, or at any rate 'play'. But it certainly is not like chess or canasta. It's more like what kittens and puppies do. Perhaps. I don't know.

* * *

D: Daddy, why do kittens and puppies play?
F: I don't know – I don't know.[19]

As indicated in the metalogue, the rules by which, as human beings, we live our daily lives are always 'undiscoverable' because they are always changing. According to Bateson's theories, they are always changing because the 'rules' that we perceive are no more than our ideas of those rules, and those very ideas themselves are always changing as we ourselves, and the contexts in which we think our ideas, are also always changing.

Our 'learning' of life, therefore, is through a constant process of play and exploration. Life is a fascinating game, an adventure, our perception and understanding of which is ever-changing and ever-deepening. As Bateson says earlier in the book: 'In the nature of the case, an explorer can never know what he is exploring until it has been explored.'[20] We must each seek to discover life for ourselves – seek to see clearly beyond our illusions of what life is.

---

[19] Gregory Bateson, *Steps to an Ecology of Mind*, Chicago: University of Chicago Press, 1972
[20] *Ibid*, chapter 1.4.1, 'The Science of Mind and Order'

In his well-known novel *Illusions*,[21] the writer Richard Bach echoes Bateson in his idea that we edit, transform and indeed create our own reality: 'This world is your imagination. Where your thinking is, there is your experience.'

Via one of the book's 'reluctant messiahs', Donald Shimoda, Bach describes the human experience thus: 'We are game-playing, fun-having creatures, we are the otters of the universe. We cannot die, we cannot hurt ourselves anymore than illusions on the [film] screen can be hurt. But we can believe we're hurt, in whatever agonizing detail we want. We can believe we're victims, killed and killing, shuddered around by good luck and bad luck.' Later on in the same passage, Shimoda adds: '... anything that's got space and time is all movie illusion ... But for a while we can learn a huge amount and have a lot of fun with our illusions, can we not?'

The understanding of life that Bach espouses in the book is summed up in two passages from a learners' manual for messiahs, entitled *The Messiah's Handbook*: 'You are led through your lifetime by the inner learning creature, the playful spiritual being that is your real self.' 'Learning is finding out what you already know. Doing is demonstrating that you know it. Teaching is reminding others that they know it just as well as you. You are all learners, doers, teachers.'

---

[21] London: W. Heinemann Ltd, 1977

This is the prize, the goal, the aim of the game of life. This is the metalogue between a conscious human being and the world: to learn who we are through our being and doing; to learn through our own heuristic experience that we are not, indeed, simply the doing.

The Purpose of the Game

Our understanding of who we are begins from the moment that we begin to understand the structure and rules of the game that we are playing in living our lives, and the skills that the game requires. In previous chapters, we have already discussed who we are not: we are neither simply our minds, nor our histories, nor our bodies.

Nor is life simply our mind's concept of it.

The purpose of the game of life is to come to discover, to explore, and to learn to live increasingly from the deepest part of ourselves: the soul level. Who we are is a continuum – from spirit to soul to mind-ego-personality to body to who we are in relation to each other and to the world around us. The more that we play the game, the more that we develop and delight in our skills at soul-living, the more we begin to live from pure consciousness, to feel, think, see, hear, act, react and experience from that place of quiet, pure, joyful clarity. The more that we experience life and express ourselves only with compassion and unconditional love, the more we have achieved the purpose of the game.

Playing the Game

The structure of the game of life is beautiful and elegantly simple: we play it by living our lives. The rules are equally simple: we learn by observing our living. The skill required is only the intention to play with awareness.

When we live life only from the level of the ego-mind – when, unknowingly, we live only through subjective experience, filtering and editing our reality and seeing only what we want to see because it conforms to our expectations – our daily experience of life can be of something chaotic, confusing, difficult, dangerous and precarious. We make the mistake of believing that the roles that we perform, what we do, what we look like, what we possess are who we are. Living at this level, we can feel that if we only have enough money, status, beauty, youth, attention, romantic love, luck, etc., etc., we will achieve security and happiness. We will do whatever we can to maintain these attributes – plastic surgery, over-work, over-competitiveness, treating colleagues and family members as we would not allow ourselves to be treated, acting from jealousy, envy, bitterness and, above all, fear. If we play the game only at this 'human' level, we begin to find that, inexorably, youth and beauty fade, our bodies creak, our minds grow tired with exhaustion, and there are always too many young guns eager to compete for our position, wealth and status. In short, when we believe that the game of life is only about competition and that the only rule is survival of the fittest, we cannot win the game; we are doomed to fail. It is very often, however, exactly at the point at which we begin to lose the mind-game that we begin to discover the nature of the real game.

Playing at the Higher Level

What do human beings tend to do when we begin to fail – when even our 'best' subjective reality seems grey, empty and hopeless? Very often, we resort to altering our perceptions of reality by self-medication or by prescription drugs. Benzodiazepines clothe the mind in fog. Alcohol numbs us into forgetting. Heroin cocoons us in a warm blanket of no-cares. Cocaine lends us the illusion of potency and vibrancy. Hallucinogens bring us revelatory, transcendent understandings of the patterns and meaning of life... which have all disappeared by the time morning comes.

We can use other equally addictive numbing mechanisms too, of course: gambling, shopping, sex, romance, beauty, to name a further few. Ultimately, what all of these drugs and activities do is protect us from the pain that is inherent within a life lived and played at too low a level: a life lived from fear. The trouble with these mechanisms, however, is that all too often they end up consuming our lives; indeed, they can become our sole reason for living.

Breaking Open

However, in these circumstances, sometimes, if we are lucky, we reach a point where we slowly begin to listen to the voice of despair that is the travelling companion of addiction, and we begin to realise that there will never be enough drugs, enough money, enough of whatever it is to which our ego-mind chooses to cleave in order to feel safe and in control. There will never be enough of these things, not because their supply is running out (it seldom does) but because we begin to grow heartsick, body-sick, of dis-ease, of half-living a numbed, confused life.

So often, it is in the moment when we reach our own rock bottom, a place so cold and bleak, so dark and silent, so hopeless, so beyond our ability to conceptualise our way out, that we are broken open by it, that we begin to hear the pure clear voice of our soul – the aspect of our being that feels only love for us. It is from that moment that we can begin to transcend our subjective reality, that we can begin to heal, that we can begin to live our life from the soul level.

Naturally, every reader will be applying a healthy and necessary scepticism to this talk of mind and soul levels, to this suggestion that your carefully honed concepts of reality might not actually be the reality within which you are living. Let us pause for a moment, then, to consider the function of the various substances, legal and illegal, a little or a lot, that most of us might have used at one point or another to alter our relationship to our reality.

Drugs alter our minds, or, rather, they pull us out of our habitual perspective of reality. Both the habitual perspective, for example depression at the chaos in our life, and the drug-altered perspective, say the calm induced by a benzodiazepine, come from and exist in our mind. Our mind is equally capable of both states, and so which is the more real? Indeed, is either of them actually 'real' at all?

The points of crisis in our lives are always gifts. This is a rule that we come to understand when we play the game of life beyond the mind level, when we play at the higher level of soul.

Learning from the Game

When we face up to an addiction, or when we lose someone or something that we love dearly, that we feel we cannot live without, we have an opportunity to learn yet another of the most important rules of the higher-level game: namely, that 'this too will pass'. We begin to sense the illusory nature of space/time 'reality'. It is in the nature of living a human life that everything that is born will die, that the transformation of energy, blossoming and decay, is constant, that fear, pain and tragedy will pass, and that so too will moments of ecstasy and joy. Playing at the higher level, we realise that ecstasy and despair are equal illusions, equally transitory, equally shifting. When we play from soul, we feel them, but we also stand back and observe the feeling. We explore, feel into the feeling and learn from it, but we know that we are not it.

Soul Reality

Living from soul is, in essence, like taking a deep belly breath before, during and after every action and reaction, so that we operate fully from the deepest place within ourselves, the place of still, quiet tranquillity, in which we sense that all can be understood and our place in the game fully revealed. In her essay 'Human Personality',[22] the French philosopher Simone Weil said of language: 'At the very best, a mind enclosed in language is in prison.' When we believe that our lives, that we, exist only at the level of concept, thought, emotion and body, we are also in a prison cell, with our faces turned to the wall, not realising that the cell door is wide open and that there is a vast, sunlit panorama beyond it.

When we allow ourselves moments of contemplation – for example, walking in a silent forest beneath the light-dappled canopy of leaves, or standing at the sea's edge listening to the pull of stones beneath the water on a summer's evening, or sitting in meditation following our own breathing – when we allow ourselves to be in silence, to feel into the deepest place within us, the place of serene stillness, we are beginning to experience our soul. As we practise living from that point, we begin to

---

[22] *Simone Weil – Selected Essays: 1934–1943*, London: Oxford University Press, 1962

experience a different perception, a different understanding of reality. Indeed, we begin to experience a deeper, sharper reality, to which we respond differently with love, compassion, clarity and peace, which betoken a total absence of fear.

This does not mean that we cease to experience challenges in our lives, or that we cease to make choices that are not the 'best' choices that we could make. Learning to live from soul is like learning to drive a car: once we are aware of soul – once we have learnt the basic skills and gained the licence – the real learning starts. We learn every time we drive: from the road, from the changing weather, from our own mistakes as a driver, from the mistakes of other drivers, etc.

'Mistakes'

When we play the game of life at the soul level, we understand that 'mistakes' are invaluable tools for learning – for gaining wisdom. Living from soul does not mean that we will not repeat mistakes; we are still very likely to fall down the same hole in the road more than once. When we live from soul, however, we discover that each time we encounter the same problem is not the repetition of a mistake. It is not that we have 'gone full circle', that we have failed to learn. Lived from the soul level, life is more like ascending a spiral staircase. Each time we encounter the 'same' problem – for example, the same emotional trigger – we are experiencing it from a higher, clearer, wiser perspective. Each time, we are increasingly able to make a wiser choice. Each encounter becomes an opportunity to grow in depth and understanding.

At the higher level of the game, there are no mistakes, only learning, with love and patience for ourselves. One of the key rules of playing the game at this level is that we let go of trying to reject our 'shadow side' – our human capacity to act, think and feel with, for example, bitterness, anger, deceit, cowardice or jealousy. We cease seeking to 'train', 'control' or 'silence' these responses that come from our lower-level ego-mind. At this level of play, we feel only an aware compassion and love for ourselves when we slip, and we reverse the slip as quickly as possible by standing back, taking that deep breath and re-centring ourselves once more in soul.

As the Ancient Greek philosopher, Heracleitus, stated, and as Gregory Bateson knew: 'Into the same river no man can step twice.' Bateson understood the importance of the relationship between ideas and context. As we play the game of life at the soul level, as we deepen in soul understanding, this becomes our context. When we encounter life issues again, our context has changed, we have changed and, hence, our responses have changed.

Oneness

In learning to live from soul, we also come to recognise our connectedness, indeed our 'oneness', with everyone and everything around us. As

Bateson described: 'Interesting phenomena occur when two or more rhythmic patterns are combined, and these phenomena illustrate very aptly the enrichment of information that occurs when one description is combined with another.'

Bateson, here, is talking about the realm of ideas, but the rich dance also occurs when we interact with each other and with the world. We are all mirrors for each other, and, as Richard Bach indicated, we are all students and teachers for each other. One of the most exhilarating rules of soul living is knowing that, for each of us, there is learning and the gaining of wisdom in every moment, with every person and in every experience that we encounter.

Creativity

As we learn to live from soul, as we become familiar with the topography of soul living, as we begin to recognise the view, we also come to understand how soul is the source of creativity and intuition, and the place from which beauty, whether it be an epiphany in art or a scientific 'eureka' moment, comes.

Who Owns Our Happiness?

A wonderful, liberating rule of the game at that soul level is that we come to know that we and we alone are responsible in every moment for our own happiness, for our own wellbeing.

The Law of Attraction, of which many of you will have read in the works of writers such as Esther and Gerry Hicks, may dictate that we attract into our lives what we are ourselves, and it may be that we attract into our lives difficult circumstances and encounters. In our living moment to moment, we may not be able to prevent people acting towards us in anger or in fear.

What we can always do, however, when we live from soul, is be who we want to meet; as the Indian philosopher Mahatma Gandhi counselled, 'Be the change that you want to see in the world.' Equally, we can always choose, in every moment, how, and from where, we react. All of the soul-level rules of the game of life are liberating. In that part of the game in which we express and receive love towards and from each other – our partners, husbands, wives, lovers, parents, children, brothers, sisters and friends – we are liberated from the pain of fear of abandonment. When we play at the soul level, we understand that we come together with those whom we love and who love us only for mutual expansion, delight and growth.

In the game of life at the soul level, we understand that the love that we are experiencing is not dependent on the other person, but on ourselves. We understand that in loving we do not owe and we do not own. 'I love you' does not mean '...and now you owe me happiness'. In love, and in all areas of our lives, the more that we play life at the soul level, the more that we come to sense and live from the natural state that the Indian philosopher and spiritual writer Jiddu Krishnamurti described as 'absolute and unconditional freedom'. Such freedom requires great discipline, and carries with it the greatest of responsibilities to act as wisely as possible in every moment.

Take the example of how we come together as lovers, and how our love can seem to become stale – our love and our lover become dull from over-familiarity. How often has each of us left a lover because we have suddenly encountered someone covered in an irresistible sheen of newness and possibility? As Krishnamurti also said: 'To live with beauty, or live with an ugly thing, and not become habituated to it requires enormous energy, an awareness that does not allow your mind to grow dull.'

Duality

One of the most fascinating prizes of living the game of life at the soul level is that living from soul removes us from duality. We come to know innately that we are the continuum of spirit – soul – mind – body – each other – the world we inhabit – the universe in which we live. We know that we are both the drop of water and the ocean. We come to know that there is no separation between us and our experience. We come to know that we are consciousness experiencing itself, and learning and growing through experience and choice, and that each 'mistaken' choice, each hardship, each ecstasy is simply an opportunity, a reminder, to realign – to re-centre ourselves at the very gold-light heart of our being: our soul.

Soul Skill Living

At the level of playing the game of life from soul, we begin to perceive an order and pattern in our lives, in the wider world and in the universe. We begin to understand that there are certain immutable universal energetic rules. We discover these, very simply, as we grow more and more to live creative, loving lives, in which we express compassion, unconditional love, non-judgment, acceptance of difference (rather than simply tolerance of it), openness, optimism, trust and a natural habit of living in the present moment, rather than in the subjective realities of an envisioned past or future. When we live from soul we choose joy, happiness, contentment. We come to embody the advice contained within chapter 44 of Lao Tzu's *Tao Te Ching*: 'Be content with what you have; rejoice in the way things are. When you realise there is nothing lacking, the whole world belongs to you.' Playing the game of life from soul means a profound awareness and acceptance that if we are not expressing these qualities in this very moment, we are working towards them.

Loving Our Bodies

The soul-level game also means that we care for our bodies, as they are the vehicles through which we experience the world. Soul playing means listening to the messages of dis-ease from our bodies, loving and nourishing them with healthy food, exercise and rest, and letting go of our fearful need to numb our experience of the world with mind-altering substances such as alcohol. It also means relinquishing our personal role in society's obsession with avoiding aging, and seeing with compassion that this obsession is nothing more than the fear of rejection and loneliness. Living from soul, we learn to perceive, embrace and rejoice in the wonderful beauty in the aging face of the wise woman – the 'crone' – and the wise man – the 'sage'.

Service

Playing the game from soul also requires us to understand and embrace the role of service: the role in which, in our thoughts, beliefs, attitudes, behaviour and actions, we intend to increase not just our own wellbeing but also the wellbeing of all around us. Our intention is the key here: the intention to consider always the wider implication of our thoughts and actions. This is because the game of life is played by all of us together, on the human and spiritual levels. As Bateson indicated, our billions of lives on this planet link together, and to the planet itself, through our personal, local, national, international, family, social, political, religious, business and cultural networks. Thus develop some of the rules for playing the game of life at the soul level.

The Nature of the Rules

For many of us, the game is one that we play unconsciously, and it is only when we begin to glimpse the rules that we begin to play the game consciously and responsibly, and to experience the joy and freedom that lie within it. Our life experiences constantly offer us the opportunity to 'remember' the rules. Often, we think that we have discovered all of them and completely understand their mechanism, but in applying them we learn still further. Indeed, one of the fundamental rules of the game of life is that there is always more to learn, and that our learning is never finished. Our knowledge and our ability to apply it simply grow ever deeper and more subtle. As Richard Bach advises in *Illusions*: 'Here is a test to find whether your mission on Earth is finished: If you're alive, it isn't.'

As we play the game, we realise that we are actually remembering the rules, rather than discovering them, because we begin to recognise them intimately as the truth; we sense an innate knowing of them at the deepest level of our being. In contrast, the 'rules' that our ego-mind works out tend to belong to the mind-level games that we play. When we come to know ourselves at the soul level, we come to remember that we have always known the soul-level rules of the game of life. As we begin to play more responsibly, more wisely, making more effective, more loving choices, we come to understand that remembering the rules is a process and that life is a process; change is a process. Each remembering might come as a sudden realisation, or it might happen step by step within the process of life.

We Are the Game

In the end, through playing the game at the soul level, we come to understand that not only are we playing the game, we are the game. We are an expression of creation experiencing and delighting in itself. We are creation, God, the universe, the Is, the life force, the source, pure consciousness – whatever name you choose – being conscious of itself. First we discover the rules and apply them to our mind games. With time, we move into a different level of play, as we remember the eternal rules and become aware that we are participating in the larger game. From there, we can have a perspective on the smaller ego-mind games.

As we come to know life and ourselves through the vehicles of our bodies, through the exercise of our minds, through our experiences, through our interactions with each other and with the world, and, above all, through learning to apply the soul-level rules, we come, more and more, to understand that we are the serene, creative peace at the heart of it all. We can call that creative peace what we wish, because the name is not the thing named. We come to understand that we are, and we are expressing, the nameless creative force that expanded the universe from a coin of dust 13.7 billion years ago and, indeed, minted the coin itself. We are expressions of that force, and, in experiencing ourselves from the still perspective of our souls through our minds, our bodies and our world, we are experiencing that force as ourselves.

Why Do We Play?

So, you might be asking, why do we have to remember all of this? Why do we have to remember the rules? Why are we not born consciously knowing them?

The following concept of incarnation could provide an answer to these questions. Before we are born, we choose to enter a particular body and life, a particular family, with a clear reason for doing so, with a particular learning purpose. One of the conditions of our human journey, however, is to forget this purpose from the moment that we are born, so that we can rediscover it, carry out our learning, on our journey. With time and exploration, we can clear away the conditioning and socialisation that we adopt through the initial stages of our journey. We can drop the limiting fears, beliefs and attitudes that most of us take on board as we move from birth towards death. All the while in this process, we are slowly expanding our conscious awareness of the higher aspects of ourselves. We start to understand and express our soul purpose more strongly, and we come increasingly to live from a perspective of love, from our divine aspect. As we do so, our purpose for this life floods back into our awareness.

Life is a dance between our human and divine perspectives. We live our lives, stand up for and look after ourselves, and we have a story, but this is a fiction. It is just a story, a subjective reality. In the end, by playing the game of life from the level of soul, we become able to let go of this concept and to exchange a life lived in duality for one lived in the reality of oneness. We come to understand the interconnectedness of all things: that I am you, and you are me. Until then, we allow our divine qualities to be tested and practised in life, often in adversity.

The Maestro

Learning to play the game of life successfully from the soul level is rather like acquiring mastery as a conductor: learning to balance the instruments in one's orchestra so that the most sublime expression of a symphony can be played. Our soul is the maestro, and our personality, mind, thoughts and emotions, actions and relationships are all the playing instruments of our lives, balanced and modulated in their playing by our soul awareness. In achieving this balance, in playing the game, we allow love to come into this world. We have the choice to overly identify ourselves with the actions that we take. In so doing, we can create a bondage from which we need to free ourselves. We can be both the doer and the witness. We pull our own strings. In our game, our divine nature keeps us standing erect. There is no owner of the game. We are the game, and we share the game, because the creative force, the universe, the Earth, you and me, we, are one.

We Are All of This

It is from the point at which we begin to embrace all of who we are – the unity of spirit-soul-mind-body – that we begin to live our lives from our highest perspective. Our personality, ego and will bind us to the world. They help us to assert ourselves, to determine our place among others, to look for opportunities in life, to act, to express choice, to move forward, to be seen and to be recognised. Our mind filters, assimilates and conceptualises our experiences in the world via our emotional and intellectual responses to those experiences. Our family and our social and cultural heritages help us to form a sense of belonging by making us feel part of a wider, deeper community, and also provide us with the liberating challenge of limits beyond which to expand.

Our body carries us for a lifetime: through the world, through all of our experiences and through all of our thoughts and emotions, seeking always to do its very best to protect and support us, even in those times when we might be doing our very best to self-destruct. Our body is a subtle, finely tuned barometer that shows us the degree of health inherent in the way in which we choose to live in the world. It is through our body that we experience the joy of vitality when we are living in a harmonious and loving way, and it is our body that tells us through the physical manifestations of disease when we are living in an imbalanced and fearful way.

In the 1980s, for example, I borrowed a considerable sum of money from my bank to speculate on the stock exchange. At first, the shares that I bought rose and rose in value, and I felt overwhelmed with exhilaration at my success. Then, of course, the 'Black Monday' market crash of 1987 occurred, and within the space of a few days my stock values not only lost all of their gains but fell far below their initial purchase price. Suddenly, I had moved from celebrating huge profits to facing likely bankruptcy. I knew that I would soon need to repay my bank loan, even though my stocks were now virtually worthless. Hoping against hope, I decided to hold on to the stocks for a few months, trying to convince myself that their value would rise again.

In response to the shock and fear engendered by the loss and by the imminent loan repayment, my body began to feel as if it were in total agony. I could not sleep, my muscles were rigid with tension, and every part of my physical self felt as if it were screaming in pain. My doctor could find no physical reason for the pain. It was there, of course, because I was holding on fearfully to the shares. I was completely full of fear, obsessively checking the stock values every few hours. I was completely rigid in my outlook, and so was my body. Nothing that I did, neither relaxation nor exercise, could alter my physical state. It was only, of course, at the point at which I finally sold my shares, at an enormous loss, that my pain disappeared almost overnight. The sale left me in considerable debt, but I was finally able to move forward, and I took on extra work until I had paid off the bank and was once more in solvency.

Each aspect of the spirit-soul-mind-body unity that we comprise helps us to deal with the world in which we find ourselves, helps us to take the initiative and to create our lives. It is the unity that forms the whole of who we each are. Our soul is an expression of, and is infused by, the creative loving force of spirit. Our mind and body are the tools through which we express our soul. Each is necessary to the other. We express who we are at the core of our being – who we are at the soul level – through the mind and body. As we come more and more to operate consciously from the soul level, we are continually sharpening these mind and body tools, fine-tuning them, making them more subtle, more successful, ever better designed for the task in hand.

As we live from soul, we become able to exchange fear for love, and confusion for clarity, in whatever situations life may bring to us, planned or sudden. We begin to develop adaptability: a supple, tensile quality that enables us to move through life with love and without fear. Sometimes, we can believe that our minds, our thoughts, our emotions, our will, even our bodies are potential saboteurs that must be controlled, but it is only when we accept their value, when we embrace their potential, that we can fully express our deepest selves. Without these tools, we cannot express ourselves, and we cannot explore the world. With them, we can express intention, we can invent, lead, change the world, and we can practise and delight in acceptance, compassion, trust, joy and unconditional love.

Soulful Living

A Loving Life or a Life Driven by the Ego-Mind?

How can we tell that we are living our life from the lower level – from the ego-mind – rather than from the soul? It is very simple: it all depends on the perspective that we choose to take. When looking at the world from the perspective of the ego-mind, we are at the mercy of what the world presents to us. From this perspective, we will mostly be looking with fear, and seeing a world in fear. From this perspective, for example, we can choose to define ourselves as a victim of our dysfunctional family, of our social class, of our cultural or religious heritage, of our troubled psyche, or of our body if it does not match magazine images of air-brushed perfection.

If we see from this perspective, our eyes are blinkered. We lack the clear, panoramic vision that comes with soul sight. We fail to feel our soul energy, and we cannot feed from our deepest self.

Experiencing and operating from our soul requires no religious faith. As previously said, the most devoted atheist, the most rigorous intellectual sceptic, can operate from soul. To do so, all that is required is simply to breathe, to be aware, to centre ourselves at the peaceful heart of our being. When we do this, we feel the profound creative force that informs our soul, the energy that gives us strength and wisdom, that enables us to love and to accept, to feel joy, compassion and unconditional love. No special connection is required, because each of us is a soul; each of us is an expression of the 'divine' energy that moves and informs the universe and everything within it.

When we allow our soul energy to prevail, we can soar above the difficulties of daily existence. We will still encounter and react to them, but we will react to them with a different understanding and attitude. All of us will remember how we felt as a child. If we had loving parents, the chances are that one of the strongest feelings that we remember is feeling safe. This enabled us to encounter daily life with an attitude of curiosity, and if the sudden appearance of something unknown unnerved us, we could hide behind our parents, be hugged, be reassured and be given an explanation that would dissolve our fear. We felt cared for, accepted for who we were, and loved, and as we grew, we grew in the knowledge that we could cope with everything that life might choose to present to us.

Sadly, not all of our childhoods will have been like this. When we live from soul, however, life can and does feel like this. We feel safe to trust in life, to love, to try, perhaps to fail, but to try again and eventually to succeed. Most of us have had difficult challenges that have helped us to grow in wisdom and courage, and to mature. Whether we have wanted or welcomed those experiences, we have faced them successfully and have learnt invaluable lessons from them, and with time, because of them, we have found growing within ourselves a more relaxed attitude towards life.

When we live from soul, challenges do not cease to come, but we know that they are there to stretch us, to make us more supple and tensile in our responses to life. Challenges addressed from soul engender and nurture within us soulful qualities such as endurance, objectivity, being fully present and aware in each moment, kindness, acceptance of difference, and, above all, unconditional love and a willingness to serve for the greater good of the whole. Love becomes a permanent feature of our lives, and fear diminishes. We come to feel at peace with the world within and without ourselves.

Our ego-mind can lack the strength, wisdom and breadth of vision to see the world from a loving perspective. We can feel unable to move ahead, overwhelmed by circumstances or by the difficulty of a challenge: for example, moving into a career for which we have more than the necessary talent, but in which we will face enormous competition. We can feel too timid to push beyond our self-perceived limitations. We can fear criticism or ridicule from our peers. Our ego-mind can become angry, bitter, selfish, making us bigoted and unwilling to help others, seeking only to better ourselves rather than to seek to be of use, too, to those around us. Our ego-mind can make us feel that we are inferior or superior to others, failing to understand that we are all absolutely equal, that we are all one.

As the ancient Chinese book of divination, the *I Ching*, says: 'It is in the depth of one's soul that one sees the Divine, the One. To know this One is to know oneself and one's place in the universe. This One is the ascending force of life in nature and in man.'[23] All self-limitations cease when we come to live from soul. From soul, we feel love and hope. As we live, and act, and feel, and think from soul more and more often, we let go of the fear of life that casts such dark shadows over the life lived from the ego-mind.

Daily Life

There is ample opportunity to link with a soulful energy, a perspective of soul in our life. Daily life offers all we need. Boredom comes to us, and we need to spice up our life; too much stimulation asks us to slow down. We face difficult and stressful situations, are in a rush. Tuning into our soulful energy, we can stay calm under pressure. We are faced with the plight of others, their misfortune, and living from soul we feel compassion. Make each day count! Someone needs encouragement, so we can reach out to her; someone pressed one of our buttons, and we can react differently: thank him for giving us the insight into what makes us squirm.

What does life throw at us on a daily level? We might lose our job or money. Over time, our beauty, prestige and power are shattered, we age, and our

---

[23] Hexagram 24: Return (The Turning Point)

social situation changes. We might quarrel with our partner, or we feel lonely being on our own. Some days, we might feel life has little to offer, as we feel uninspired and lack hope for the future. Maybe we feel trapped in a rat race and we are trying to keep up with the Joneses. Our family needs more commitment; maybe there is a sick relative and we do not feel up to that job.

Challenges will be different for all of us, but we will face similar trials at any given time in our life. Today we might feel on top of the world because life went our way. We feel ecstatic and want to hang on to this feeling, but after a short while it already begins to elude us. On the next day, we might feel down and empty within ourselves. Why are we not able to hold on to positive feelings from yesterday? When we connect with success and positive feelings on the ego level only, it is superficial. We need to look at life in a more dispassionate way. If we fail to do so, we make ourselves vulnerable to the ups and downs in life. Like a leaf in the wind, we are tossed around with the feeling of not being in control of our life. And maybe we are not in control. When going within, we feel reassured about life, even though we might not completely be or feel in charge.

Living from the point of soul helps us see life with dispassion. Daily life challenges us to connect to within, to soul, and to embody soulful qualities. This way we can overcome our emptiness. At the end of the day, we hope to feel this day has been successful and in some way counted. With our attitude we make it so. When we choose an attitude of soul, of love, when we quickly link with soul, we make the day worthwhile, independent of what it has been like. Have you lived today from a perspective of soul, of love? When you do so, you are better equipped to deal with daily changes in your experience of and feelings towards life.

How do we link with a soulful perspective, a quality of love in our life?

Listen

In the hectic rush of modern life, we tend not to listen to within, being mainly focussed on the outside. But life, our soul, asks us to pay attention. This can be via a dream, an insight, a thought, a feeling, or just something that is sent to us from the outside but leads to a feeling inside of wanting to pay attention.

Ericka

Ericka, a French national, was made redundant from her last job. She had been working successfully in sales for a number of years, but her company was taken over and her position was made redundant. Ericka received a good redundancy package and enjoyed time off work for a couple of months. She felt she did not want to go back into sales again, as her last job had been stressful. Ericka felt it had taken a lot of energy to perform the job. After some time, she became restless and felt she needed a routine again to get a new perspective in her life. She did all the usual things jobseekers do, sending out her CV, applying for jobs. As the world was coming out of a strong recession, permanent jobs were not as easy to come by as they had been a few years previously. Therefore, Ericka was happy to consider a temping job to get back into a routine while looking for a permanent job.

Ericka had been brought up in a strict family environment. Her father was a law-abiding citizen who seemed never to have strayed from the path of living an honest, decent and straightforward life. From a young age, Ericka was told to work hard and always to respect people. Her father, who respected authority, instilled a sense of duty in her. In particular, she was to respect people in positions of authority. All of her young working life, Ericka felt somehow awkward around her managers. She felt she had to behave correctly, to be obedient and follow instructions, to be respected and liked. Sometimes, it felt as if she were fearful of people in power and authority. Ericka had, however, worked on this issue with counselling and other methods, as she felt this kind of feeling would hold her back in her life. As Ericka was very intuitive, she paid particular attention to her dreams.

She was contacted by an agency to work as a long-term temp for a telemarketing company, phoning French firms to offer them certain products and services. Knowing how difficult a job like this was, she flatly refused it. A day later, however, she was contacted by another agency about the same job and company. Amused, she refused the job again. But when yet another company phoned her later in the day, offering the same position, Ericka listened to the agency selling her this job. She was amused and somehow surprised that this opportunity would come around a third time. Was this company desperate to find someone who spoke French and having trouble in succeeding? Or was a deeper issue at hand here? As an intuitive person with lots of life experience, Ericka did not believe in coincidences. She considered the agency's suggestion to work for a couple of weeks to see how it went. She could then decide whether she wanted to continue in this job.

She accepted the temp job and was thoroughly trained in the area of networking technology for three days, as the telemarketing company wanted to make sure she had enough background knowledge when talking to French companies. Phoning the companies was a frustrating job. Her data was incomplete, and she had to find decision makers first. Often, the company receptionist she phoned was not willing to give her the name of the responsible person to talk to. When she got through to the right person in the end, that person was often not interested, or she found that the company already had a networking solution from another provider in place. Ericka had known before that this might happen, but still felt she might be responsible for not generating enough leads. On top of that, her programme manager did not listen to her concerns. He put undue pressure on her to generate more leads. He even checked when she started and finished work, as he had to authorise her hours to be paid.

Ericka was beginning to wonder why she had accepted the job. Maybe her intuition was wrong and this job would not lead to anything in terms of learning or moving forward in her life. After two weeks in the job – the time she had given herself to see how it went – she had a vivid and lucid dream. She dreamt that she was flying in the air and showing others how easily and beautifully she was flying. This dream stayed with her in the morning, and she reminded herself to look it up after her work.

When she arrived at work, her manager confronted her again about the hours she had worked. She felt pressurised and queasy in her stomach. At the same time, she was angry that her manager was talking to her as he did: in a reproachful and blaming manner. She kindly, but strongly, informed him that she disliked the way he talked to her and he was not to talk to her like this again. On top of that, she was doing the best she could in her job; after all, she had contacted a good number of companies in France. As she had ample sales experience and applied herself, it was not her fault that the number of leads was not higher than it was. She told her manager there could be a number of factors of why the number of leads was low. Many companies, in particular decision makers, were on vacation in France in August. Furthermore, the quality of the leads was lower than expected, and many companies either just were not willing to talk to telemarketers or had a solution in place already.

Once Ericka had told her manager all this, she felt much better. She also felt her time in this company had come to an end. She kindly told her manager she would no longer be available for the job and left an hour later after tying up some loose ends. Ericka felt elated. When she came home, she quickly checked her dream about flying on the web. Here was what she found under dreammoods.com:

Flying dreams fall under a category of dreams known as lucid dreams. Lucid dreams occur when you become aware that you are dreaming. Many dreamers describe the ability to fly in their dreams as an exhilarating, joyful, and liberating experience.

If you are flying with ease and are enjoying the scene and landscape below, then it suggests that you are on top of a situation. You have risen above something. It may also mean that you have gained a different perspective on things. Flying dreams and the ability to control your flight is representative of your own personal sense of power.

Ericka realised she had finally overcome the fear and intimidation she felt from someone in authority. While her father had meant well, she had suffered from this all her life. With all her work for transformation and change, she strongly felt she had now overcome this detrimental feeling in her life. Her dream had indicated this. The situation life had presented her with shortly afterwards, on her arrival at work, had allowed Ericka to overcome her fear and embrace her own power. It had taken her such a long time to arrive at this point, but Ericka felt elated. She had followed the reminder from her soul, which had led to understanding. The job she had hesitated in accepting was instrumental to her change. This job had allowed her to prove her own power to herself. She was pleased she had listened to the cue her soul had sent to her so persistently two weeks ago.

After this experience, Ericka realised a sales job was not too bad a job after all, given the experience she had had with telemarketing. A sales job was more holistic and rewarding in terms of lead generation, follow-up and closure of the business. There was less cold calling, too. A sales job was better paid, and with her experience she should be in demand for such a job. Ericka decided to focus her job search on sales jobs again. Two days later, she was contacted by an agency for a sales job with an international company. She was invited for an interview and was offered the job shortly afterwards. Not only was the job only about five miles away from her home, she also found she was promoted to a managerial job after a year. Ericka had listened to life, to her soul and intuition, and had learnt a few valuable lessons on top of getting a good job. Life presents to us what we need. We need to take time to listen to life; when we do so, we honour the process of living a soulful life.

Go with the Flow of Life

Life directs us towards what we need or want to do at any given time, if we care to listen. As souls, we speak to ourselves. Maybe we just want to indulge in some activity, but deep down we know there is something we have postponed a few times that needs doing. Somehow, intuitively, we feel it is time to follow what life dictates to make things easier, and our higher awareness speaks to us. This can be as a feeling that will not go away, or something we promised ourselves to do nagging us at the back of our mind, or a close friend kindly reminding us.

Whatever was postponed – a tax declaration, overhauling our CV to find a better job, an unpleasant phone call we need to make to someone whom we find irritating, the need to familiarise ourselves with a new gadget we bought when we dread reading the manual etc. – once done will make us feel the better for it. The tax declaration is done in a few hours, and we feel better. The CV is rewritten and we can expect better chances in our job hunt. The unpleasant phone call allowed us to show compassion and kindness to someone else. The gadget makes our life easier.

Sometimes, on the other hand, we tell ourselves we ought to do something, but have the urge to clean or tidy our flat instead. Once we have cleaned and tidied, we might feel tidier and cleaner within ourselves. That cleansing feels like a new beginning, a change; it allows us to gain a new perspective, and we feel more equipped to move forward in our life afterwards. During the cleaning and tidying up of our surroundings, a new perspective takes shape all of a sudden. Instead of laboriously working on finding a new perspective on life, we indulged in cleaning our flat. Our outer cleansing tidied up our inner life, our thoughts. A complicated situation seemed to become simple, and an avenue we did not see before showed up in front of us very clearly.

Life is a mirror image of us. We project our wishes onto life, and life mirrors responses to our actions and thoughts. We constantly form new perspectives – as within, so without – and sometimes it takes an inner cleansing to make life clearer on the outside. Once we have followed our soul impulse, we often feel gratitude for having done so.

This impulse can also entail simply 'being' instead of 'doing'. In our hectic times, we are full of plans of 'must's and 'should's. If we indulge our thinking like this, we can come to feel sluggish and full of guilt, as the tasks we set ourselves are many. However, 'being' needs to be respected on a regular basis. We might want to go somewhere, be active, but today we feel as if we should just sit and rest. This is a clue we give to ourselves: our soul is telling us to take time for recuperation. This does not have to be an excuse for not being active with regard to something we loathe. We can be aware of that and overcome barriers to inaction, if action is what is needed, but we need to heed the call for rest, for simply being, sitting, resting: for listening to ourselves, letting go, instead of working, at least once in a while. As busy professionals or parents we invite stress, potential burnout, irritation at least, when we do not listen to our inner guidance for rest. Life might become a list of jobs we are unwilling to do. It might feel a burden, a task we cannot achieve. Listen to your weary body, to the guidance from your soul, to your cluttered mind and emotions of tiredness. They tell you when it is time to just be. When we listen, when we go with the flow of life, we are living a soulful life. Our soul communicates via our feelings and our intuition. When we listen carefully, we are able to create balance in our life.

Balance

From a perspective of soul, we are inspired to seek balance in our life. We create balance when we look at our world from our perspective of/as soul. When we live from our soulful energy, connecting with love, we will take action to re-establish balance in our life.

Imagine you lose your job. The daily structure you have known is lost. There are no more daily tasks and challenges. In the beginning, you might be ecstatic, as you have time to sleep long, rest, read; you have the freedom to do whatever you want. After a while, though, despite this freedom, you connect with an emotion of restlessness and agitation. Maybe this change has come into your life, or you brought it about, albeit unconsciously, because the time for change, for a different challenge has arrived. So you set out to find a different, more challenging or more fulfilling job. You might remember how you moaned about your last job and smile at yourself. It is dawning on you how important a daily challenge and routine has been in your life, how you valued the communication with colleagues and the daily challenge to test, experience and embody your human qualities: enthusiasm, perseverance, joy, insight into business, focus, to name but a few. Working with others might have given you the feeling of being alive and using your talents.

Often it is when we lack something that we realise what we had or could have. With a lack of challenges, our life might feel dull and uninspiring to us. A lack of money can spur us on to create more abundance. The absence of a romantic relationship makes us join a dating website, or we look for love from within. An absence creates a vacuum that we want to fill; we want balance. Balance can mean different things at different times in our life. With too much work and stress we yearn for rest and quiet; too many challenges make us think about a more sedate life. Soulful living means living a life in balance.

A lack of internal balance is mirrored on the outside. I remember a time of strong personal upheaval many years ago. Around that time, my house was burgled, a few months later my car was vandalised, and I was surprised to be in a road accident a few months after that. In hindsight, I realised my internal imbalance, my turmoil, was mirrored on the outside. We all have experienced the feeling of internal turbulence when a disaster struck, war occurred; external imbalance is mirrored within.

Choose wisely to create today with balance in your life! If you sit on your couch all day, you will feel stuffy and tired. If you over-exert yourself with sport and activities, you might feel haggard and driven. It is you who knows what balance will look like for yourself. There is no perfect recipe for the right balance in life. How do you know what balance looks like for yourself, what you need? Sit quietly, breathe slowly, focus on your heart centre, and ask yourself this question. Doing so, you are looking at yourself, your world from a soulful perspective. Listen to yourself, listen to your soul, and the answer will come to you. It might just sound like a whisper, but you will know. When we look at our world from the perspective of soul, our questions will be answered. Sometimes, it might take longer, and we might need to sit with it regularly for a while. A short walk, drinking a coffee around the corner, letting the world go by can lead to inspiration from your soul. Sometimes, a friend might call, or you may feel like calling them as you have felt isolated for a few days; follow your intuition.

When we are out of balance, our struggle to re-establish it can keep us from living and experiencing life as it is now. Our attention is drawn to a feeling inside that stems from being out of kilter. This might be boredom as we have not challenged ourselves enough, or it might be the opposite. Many of us will remember a time when all we wanted was to rest and sleep. Our mind was hurting, our body ached with pain, and our emotions felt dumb. We had overdone it, allowed too much stress into our life, and our daily routine felt stale and uninspiring. All we could do was rest. At other times, we might have read too much, or spent too much time in the office or at home and too little time out in nature. Perhaps we needed to run to tire ourselves physically, and having done so we felt more relaxed and at peace.

When our attention is occupied with our feeling of imbalance, we do not pay attention to life as it is now. We miss the experience of living in the present, the joy that derives from that. This in turn can throw us out of kilter, and we unbalance ourselves even further until eventually sufficient balance is restored to help us to participate in life again. During such periods in our life, we might find it difficult to draw up new schemes for our lives. This is not the time to consider difficult decisions, to allow too much change and upheaval. It is when we have re-balanced ourselves again that we can make life-changing decisions.

Often, however, a life-changing decision itself can restore balance in our lives.

David

David came from a middle-class family that considered financial and material success to be the epitome of life. He had been a high achiever from a young age, at school, in sports, at university. He finished university as the best in his year and was offered a job as a financial accountant with an international company. Gradually, he climbed the professional ladder. He married in his twenties and had two children.

David worked about 12 hours a day, often at weekends as well. He tried to instil a sense of achievement in his young children, Craig and Joshua. Both listened but seemed to have their own way of seeing the world. His wife, Alexia, saw her role as removing all mundane obstacles from David's life; she looked after the children and supported David emotionally. They lived in a very big house in a sought-after area.

One day, Joshua, the youngest son, complained about pain and dizziness and, at only ten years old, was diagnosed with cancer. David could not believe that this could have happened to him, a person who had everything under control.

Joshua's doctors advised that he needed to be operated on quickly and would need a year of rest and recuperation. Until that time, David had been a 'weekend father': work always came first. All of a sudden, he realised that he could have lost his son and that he still could, when he had not spent much time with him at all. All David's concepts about life, like the importance of success and abundance, seemed to be crumbling.

From this point, David began to understand that he had not looked at life from a deeper, less material viewpoint. He had not listened to that more fundamental aspect of life, and a life balance was missing. David came to feel that if he continued that way, he would finally face a burnout. He had not listened to his wife either and had not taken time to 'smell the roses'. Alexia had always felt that she and her family would be safe. As long as love could be present and be expressed, Alexia believed, life would respond accordingly.

We might be enticed to see the illness as a sign sent by life to pay attention. It certainly caught David's attention. David talked to his wife, and they decided to sell the big house, in order to gain more financial independence, and move into a smaller one. He also decided to take a sabbatical to have more time for his family and himself.

It was not easy. David craved the excitement of work, the adrenaline rush that came from making decisions. At work he felt influential; he had a say. After a while, however, his nervous system adapted; he felt calmer and enjoyed the time spent with his family. Joshua did recover, and David felt grateful for the time he had had with Joshua and Craig.

After a year, the changes within David became obvious. He had connected with a softer, more spontaneous part within himself. He laughed more often. In the time spent with the boys, he refilled his heart, and he came to feel more youthful within himself. David decided to work part-time as a financial adviser. Alexia wanted to work as a nurse part-time as well, so that both could work and look after the children.

Sometimes, life presents us with events we have to pay attention to. Depending on the event and our belief, we might think we have brought about this event ourselves. Our soul has done this from a creative point of view, or life has conspired on our behalf, and, without an understanding of the how and why, we can just marvel at the perfection of it all. These events help us change our lives. Once we listen, we can restore balance. A strong event can entice us back into going along with the flow of life; we listen, we take action, and life can take a turn for the better.

A Step at a Time

Sometimes life might seem to be overwhelming us in some way. Soulful living, mainly living from a soul perspective of love, encourages us to live our life a step at a time. When we are living from a balanced soul perspective, often our next step in life becomes obvious and we can follow it easily.

We might plan our life, but our plan seems grand and unachievable. We have a dream we want to follow, but the dream seems enormous. Because of this, we might give up easily. While we can see the end result, we do not know how to go about achieving it. Maybe we want to change ourselves – perhaps we want to lose weight, for example – but we fail to take action, as the change seems overwhelming.

Jane

Jane worked with people who had strong allergies or general dietary problems. She trained in several therapy forms, such as kinesiology, and had a good reputation for achieving remarkable results. Her clients were often overweight; they felt sluggish and had skin irritations. Some of them had not worked for years and, wanting to change their lives, had come to Jane for advice and treatment.

After a thorough examination, Jane usually prescribed a tough regime of change. With her testing, she confirmed which food items were not advisable for the client to eat. Often the foods to be avoided were wheat and dairy products. Together with her advice on foods to be avoided, Jane also prescribed a regime of walking and exercising. Those who followed her advice underwent strong, positive and remarkable changes. Not only did these clients lose weight, but they also felt more alive and more positive, and some were able to get back into a job for the first time in years, especially those who suffered from chronic fatigue syndrome.

This seemed to apply to about 50% of her clients. The other 50%, however, felt unable to follow her strict prescribed regime. They felt overwhelmed; whatever Jane prescribed for them was just too much. Jane did realise some of her clients were unable to cope with so many changes at once, but she did not want to change her approach and was happy to work with the other 50% of her clients. Her bookings often dropped off dramatically after the initial consultation. Those who felt overwhelmed did not come back after the results of the testing were out and Jane had prescribed her regime. Jane could have helped the reluctant 50% by being more flexible in her approach, but she was just not willing to change or adapt it.

When life seems to overburden us, we need to remember we only have to take a step at a time. It is this one step we need to take now. With regard to Jane's clients, they could have cut out one food item first, instead of all of them at once. Their recovery might have taken a bit longer, but they would have been able to start, instead of giving up before even trying. Once the first step had been achieved, like cutting out dairy, the next step could have been taken, like tackling wheat products.

When we take the first step, the next one often shows itself; it becomes obvious. Our body, our intuition might tell us. Our soul talks to us via our body, emotions or intuition. Instead of struggling to find the right or perfect solution, we can just follow life by taking the next logical step when it becomes apparent. Each journey starts with the first step. Once that step is taken, the next one shows itself, and we can take that. Before we know it, simply by having taken the next obvious steps, we find ourselves approaching the finale of our task. This way it has been so much easier than we thought it would be.

Some of us go through rapid and extreme change. Maybe someone died, or we have a sudden realisation, an epiphany. For most of us, though, change is subtle and occurs during all our life in a way we almost do not notice. We might change one aspect of ourselves, then the next obvious aspect, then the next. One day, we suddenly realise, change has happened. We made it happen – not with a fanfare, not by labouring over change, but by just taking a step at a time.

When we feel overwhelmed by necessary changes, by a task, by a plan to follow, we are advised to cut them all down into bite-sized amounts. Once the first chunk has been digested, we have room for the next one. Taking a step at a time allows for balance. When we attempt to jump the steps, we might lose our balance – like a juggler who tries to juggle too many balls at once.

Soulful Living and Nature

Being, walking and resting in nature help us to view life from a soulful perspective. For a while, we might have looked at life from a perspective of fear, seeing life from our ego and personality alone, but, as many of us will have realised, once we are in nature, we can feel healing. This can feel like a healing of our busy mind or our stressful emotions, and nature can have an effect on these things, but it is ultimately a healing of our perspective. We look at nature with the eyes of soul, and we see life with a soulful perspective again.

We find the elements of nature outside towns and cities. Most of us live in cities nowadays, and we do not always have the opportunity to walk, to be in nature. Exposing ourselves to the elements of nature, however, can help us to see ourselves, and life, from a perspective of soul again.

Rain

Many years ago, a friend and I were working in a garden. We had been in the garden for a few hours, and had thoroughly enjoyed working with the soil. For a while, dark clouds had been gathering over our spot, and we expected strong rain to bless the garden. All of a sudden, we had the idea of stripping down naked to let the rain pour over us. We felt this would have a refreshing and cleansing effect. The neighbours might be irritated, but we were used to this anyway. When the rain started, we quickly stripped, the rain started to pelt down, and we felt the warm summer rain on our naked skin. Both of us were laughing with joy, as the sensation was spectacular. Tired as we were from several hours of work in nature, we felt utterly refreshed and cleansed by the rain.

Unless we live in a desert region, for many of us rain is readily available to help us wash away our sorrow, our thoughts and irritations. It does not cost anything; we just need to expose ourselves to the cleansing effect rain can have on us. When we are in the rain, we can imagine it washing away our negative emotions, our troubling thoughts. We can imagine the rain to have a certain cleansing colour to support the effect. We can make such an occasion a soulful exercise of cleansing. With our mind and feelings, our attitude and soulful perspective, this chosen colour, together with the rain, can wash away everything we need to let go of at that moment. We can see ourselves in a different, cleaner colour afterwards. We might have seen whatever the rain has drained away in dark, brown and murky colours, whereas afterwards we will probably see a more uplifting colour around us. Even drying ourselves with a towel afterwards can serve the same purpose; with the towel we wash/dry off any residual energy we do not want to keep.

Remember who you are! Quantum physics indicates that we are made of minute pieces of energy, and that with our observation we change our reality. When we imagine such a cleansing from deep within, there is a strong chance it will happen. Can all our deep ingrained problems be washed away like this? Probably not, as this might need a different approach, but we can certainly cleanse away irritating thoughts and feelings, or tiredness from the office. Such a cleansing helps us to see ourselves, and life, with a perspective of soul again, and in doing so we can also look into deeper aspects within that need healing and change over time.

The Wind and Cold

George used to suffer from intense migraines. When they approached, he had to lie in a darkened room to wait until his pain subsided. Most of the time, he was not able to work and he had to vomit. Sometimes, the pain in his head was so strong that he had to walk up and down his bedroom, as the movement helped him overcome his nausea and pain for a while. George had changed his diet; he did not eat any cheese or chocolate any more, nor did he drink any red wine. This had helped to a certain extent, but his strong migraines remained.

One winter on a windy day, George felt a migraine attack approaching. Instead of lying down, he felt he should walk outside in the wind. It was a cold winter day, and the wind was very strong.

George had always loved the wind. So he started walking. While the intense walk warmed his body, the very cold wind seemed to cool his head. He knew from experience that cooling his head with a cold towel had alleviated his pain in the past, but walking in the cold wind was a better and new experience for George. Walking distracted him from his pain, and the cold wind cooled his head enormously. After two hours' walk, George felt his migraine subside, and a deep peace came over him. It was only when, after a few years, George realised he had to connect with his feelings, with a deeper level of himself, that his migraines eventually disappeared altogether. With meditation and healing, relaxation and letting go of his fears, George let go of his migraines.

In our modern times, many of us suffer from thought-overload. We are bombarded with facts. We think incessantly, we process information, and our thoughts obscure our emotions. Wind has an intense effect of cleansing. Tornados break down trees and houses. While they can have devastating effects on a community by destroying homes and nature, this also has a cleansing effect. Stronger houses are being built, and younger, stronger and more flexible trees are being planted afterwards. Strong winds have a purging effect. Autumn has always been my favourite season because of its strong winds. When walking in the wind, we can imagine the wind around our head and body pushing away any negativity. The wind can enter our head and wash out troubles, pushing away our sorrow, even if only for a short time. When strong wind pushes against our bodies, we can visualise it pushing away our negative emotions and clearing our heads. With a clearer head and more positive emotions, we regain the strength to live life more creatively and peacefully.

The cold can numb our pain. The hot sun can melt away our stubbornness, or old and resistant feelings. When we allow the elements of nature to help us cleanse away layers of thoughts and ingrained feelings, we regain a perspective of soul. By connecting with nature, we feel our connectedness with the Earth, the universe and creation. This in turn helps us see ourselves, and life, from a soulful perspective again.

Our soul reminds us of our divine origin. We guide ourselves from this perspective. Often, however, we are insensitive to this reminder and guidance. Our thoughts and attention are trapped by the daily drama of existence, and we allow ourselves to be overly distracted by trivia, the media and others. Messages from our soul are not listened to, as we are distracted. These messages are often subtle: an intuition or inkling, a sense of something we cannot make concrete yet, a feeling of déjà vu. Sometimes, though, we receive a clear idea, a definite knowing, all depending on the strength of our soul perspective. When we allow the elements of nature to free us, even if only temporarily, as described, we open ourselves up again to a soulful perspective. Often, a direct approach can make all the difference: ask your soul for guidance.

Soulful Living in the Practice of Life I

Ask Your Soul for Guidance

We can all get lost in life. Sometimes, we feel helpless and we fail to come up with an idea, a solution for a problem or situation we are faced with. Of course, there is the option of asking our family and friends for help. That can be the right course of action, but sometimes they are busy, and they have their own particular way of approaching life, problems and situations. Overall, we might also feel we want to become more reliant on ourselves and work with our own inner resources. We can ask ourselves for advice, ask our soul (or we might call it the universe or God, whatever we prefer), and, if we are attentive, we will notice the solution or advice coming to us. Any problem has a built-in solution. It is up to us to trust in this. If we ask for advice inside and/or outside ourselves, the advice will surely come. There is no need to tune in, relax or sit in meditation, although that can be a sensible approach as well.

An 80-year-old friend of mine is a trance medium. Whenever Sheila needs some help, she asks her 'fellas', as she calls them, for advice. Some years ago, Sheila wanted some work done on her old house. She wanted to have her fireplace sorted out, but only had about £600 to spend on the work. She phoned several builders and specialists for quotes, but no one seemed to be willing or able to do this job for less than £1000. 'Hello, fellas,' she said, 'I need your help. Please show me how I can get the fireplace fixed for a maximum of £600.'

Knowing that she had stated her wish to the universe and that an answer would invariably come, she went about her daily life and forgot about this. A few days later, at the college where she took lessons in painting, she saw a notice board. She strongly felt she should have a look at it. On the board was a note by a trainee builder who was offering his work at reduced rates. He needed a piece of work to show for the completion of his training. Sheila phoned him up, and he came round with his father. He said he was able to do the job for £400, given the time involved in breaking down and renewing the fireplace. He promised to check on the cost of materials and to let her know. A day later, the trainee builder phoned and told her the cost would be £200, so the overall cost would be £600. Sheila asked him to do the job, and was very pleased with it. Two years later, she took out some money from her house for extensive refurbishment, and it was this builder whom she contacted. He was able to do an environmentally friendly job in good time and at fair cost.

Sheila has always worked this way: she asks for guidance, a solution, and, as she confirmed to me, to this day she has always received an answer. We do not have to struggle with a problem in our life and think it is completely up to us to find the solution. We can ask for a solution, an approach, a method, whatever we need. Once we have asked our soul, the universe, our higher self or God, we can let it go and expect an answer. This is not about finding the right numbers to win the lottery. Life is a playground that helps us to wake up to our divine potential. Without challenges, we would not have any incentive to dig deeper, to find out what we are capable of.

An answer can come in many ways. A friend might be talking about something in particular, and a sudden thought might appear pointing towards a solution. We might come across a book or article that gives us an insight into our situation. Perhaps something is mentioned on TV or radio that gives us an idea, or we receive a phone call from someone who offers us a product or solution we need. We can also have a sudden insight, we can remember something we have truly forgotten, or an intuition we have might urge us to talk to someone in particular and, on doing so, we might realise this person knows the solution to our problem. Alternatively, we might suddenly have a strong feeling about a course of action to take. We can either have a solution at hand, or find that our insight or external advice starts a process that leads to a solution. Trust is needed in all this, and an openness to life: a curiosity to pursue whatever comes to us, without dismissing it. If we ask for help sincerely, and surrender to our need for help, an answer will definitely come.

Stay Open to Life

We might think we know what is going to happen in our life. As a creator of our life, exercising free will, we might feel we determine the direction of our life completely. While this can be the case at times, it also helps to stay open to what life brings to us. We are responsible for our life, but are we not co-creators? We can choose to believe in a co-creative process of life, and we can make that our paradigm for life. Life can be seen as a co-operative process between our human and spiritual dimensions. On the human level, we have desires, hopes and aspirations. Often, we take cues from what is considered appropriate in life. We aim to have a career, maybe a family, a social life, friendships, social status and entertainment.

This is only natural, as we are able to shape ourselves with and through the life we have chosen. Life offers us the opportunity to develop our human and divine qualities, like trust and love in all its expressions. We develop these with life when all goes smoothly, as well as through life when we seem to struggle. Sometimes, however, we as soul send reminders to ourselves to adjust our journey. Maybe there is a path ahead we cannot see yet. Following it, though, will assist us in seeing life from a soul perspective again. The qualities we will develop on this path will allow us to shift our perspective; we will see life from within more strongly and re-discover our divine origin. This path might help us to correct a current journey, to adjust its direction. It might also bring about what we want in terms of our desires quicker and more easily.

Frank

In Germany many years ago, I befriended a young man who was doing his national service in the German army. Frank came from humble origins; his parents considered themselves to be working class. When Frank decided to stay with the German army for two years, instead of only the 15-month national draft period, they were very proud of him.

Frank applied himself to his job admirably. After a few months, he was asked whether he would like to take part in training to become an officer. Frank went for it and excelled at every level. After two years, he was made lieutenant, and he followed an accelerated career path. Before the end of his two-year service, Frank had already decided to extend his service to four years as a next step.

Frank's parents and friends felt confident Frank would become a career officer in the army. Life seemed to indicate that he would. Frank seemed to be a born soldier and leader. He was popular with his fellow officers and respected by his troops, and he excelled at many things. His mind was alert, he learnt quickly, and he developed true leadership qualities at a young age. After less than four years, he was promoted to first lieutenant. At this stage, Frank was only 22 years old, as he had joined the army at 18 years of age. He was expected to take the next courses and become one of the youngest captains in the army.

Everyone, including Frank, saw a clear career path ahead. Several events in his life, however, then shattered his belief in the right course of career in his life. A close friend died young, having developed a cancer that was not curable. In his duties, Frank was also exposed to the misery of others' lives when he took part in a restructuring programme for people who had lost all their belongings in a disaster. Frank was deeply moved and felt compassion. He had come to a point in his life where he connected more strongly with his feelings, despite the no-nonsense regime in the army. Officers were not expected to show feelings and compassion, at least at that time about 30 years ago. As lives were potentially at stake in a combat situation, compassion, hesitation, deeper thinking were not considered conducive to the survival of a soldier. A soldier had to follow orders.

Frank discussed his dilemma with his non-soldier friends and, almost imperceptibly, within a few months, went through a deep transformation. On the surface, life seemed to follow the expected path, and Frank did his duty. Underneath this, however, Frank pondered about his life and future. Shortly before the end of his four years in the army, Frank decided to become a male nurse.

When Frank told his commanding officer he would not extend his service and follow a career in the army, his commanding offer was surprised, but not shaken. After all, this happened occasionally. While Frank could go far in his career, his commanding officer had seen other officers crumble, have second thoughts.

The idea of Frank wanting to become a male nurse, however, threw his commanding officer completely. How could an officer, a first lieutenant, decide to train as a male nurse? Frank's parents and colleagues expressed a similar reaction. So too did the drafted soldiers he commanded, even though they were more naturally sceptical about the army. As an officer there were other career options outside the army, such as a position in a company or as a civil servant, but a nurse? Frank's commanding officer asked Frank to reconsider, but Frank had made up his mind.

His training as a soldier paid off nicely, as Frank was organised, disciplined and used to applying himself. He was not squeamish, as he had seen blood before. He possessed patience and a quick mind. Frank enjoyed his training enormously and never looked back. He passed his examinations with flying colours. At the age of 27, two years after he had finished his training as a nurse, Frank decided to study medicine. While it took until his mid-thirties before he could practise as a doctor, he kept going and became an excellent doctor. Asked why he did not stay in the army to become an army doctor, he laughed. When he had made his decision to leave the army, he had had no plans to become a doctor at all. Being a male nurse had seemed enough of an ambition.

Life can throw a spanner in our works. Almost like a secret scheme, events occur that make us stop in our tracks and look more closely. These events stir deep feelings and make us think. All of a sudden, we are confronted with feelings and thoughts that seem to come out of nowhere. Life and our soul always remind us to pay attention. A new path ahead is the better one for our development. As we might be strongly set in our ways, we need shaking up. Our complacence and certainty must be challenged. We leave a certain path and enter uncharted territory.

We might want to resist despite the obvious and follow what we have planned for ourselves. In this, we might even succeed for a while, but we all know life can and will surprise us. It is when we pay attention and are open to the course of life that we feel, see and understand. All of a sudden, we can see the illusion of our plans. We connect with a different path and purpose, and this path develops more divine qualities, such as Frank's growing compassion. Stay open to life; it teaches us! Clues are given, and we can follow them. In doing so, we learn to trust and go with the flow of life. This can go along with success and fulfilling our desires, and it often does. When we are open and align ourselves with a deeper, often hidden, purpose, we can become more successful and fulfilled at the same time. When we listen to our intuition, when we pay attention to our feelings and to what life presents to us, we allow life to guide us. We live a more soulful life.

Slowing Down and Resting

Soulful living is about smelling the roses at least once in a while. If we are on a rollercoaster, life is flying by. Slowing down our pace gives us time to be in and feel into life. Our speed of life in the present day has increased enormously, in aspects including how we feed our bodies and the decrease in the amount of rest we allow ourselves. Soulful living is about listening to life. When we slow down, we can deal with our emotions more compassionately; we can bring structure to our incessant thoughts; we can pay attention to our body more easily and heal ourselves.

Rush, rush, rush seems to be the order of the day. We rush to work. We rush to escape from work with entertainment, instead of by being with ourselves. We bolt down our food. We chase money. We chase happiness through outside events and stimuli. As a wise woman told me once, 'less is more'. All things need to be in proportion, and we need a slower pace. When we slow down our daily activities, we live more attentively. Maybe we can even find wisdom in the boredom we encounter. When we miss a train, we can catch another one later; when we stop rushing, we can find peace inside ourselves.

When we tire ourselves physically, we affect our mental and emotional states, and in turn our attitude and behaviour. Equally, we affect our physical health when we churn our emotions and thoughts in reaction to others: when we do not apply a check on the number of negative thoughts in our internal dialogue, allowing too many to accumulate.

In many cases, this process happens subconsciously and we are not aware of our thoughts, many of which result from childhood programming. We just do not pay attention to our thinking. When we choose to refocus and pay attention, over and over again, we make ourselves aware of these tiger traps. We can wake ourselves up from unconscious programming! We can become aware of our fearful thinking and make a choice for love at that very moment. A friend of mine uses the mantra 'I choose love' repeatedly in her mind when she is walking to town, or when she feels she is giving in to drama and negative thinking. After doing this for a while, she feels much more peaceful, with a calmer mind. Each moment of choosing love forms a period of 'love'-thinking. When we pay attention and make a choice for love repeatedly, our periods of a calmer mind will become longer. To do this, we need to slow down and also rest. When our body is at rest, we are more successful at training our mind, and when we pay attention to our mind, slowing down and changing our way of thinking, our body will follow suit.

Of course, it is more difficult to make positive choices, to think positively, when we feel the effects of an illness, or when we grieve. In such a state, it is more difficult to believe in any positive change.

Fear can hold us in a vice-like grip. Breaking free can also be especially difficult when our body is physically manifesting dis-ease. How can we overcome that? We can overcome it by our intention to pay attention (see below), rather than trying to run away from our pain or dis-ease. When we attempt to avoid pain, such as grief, or when we do not want to give our body the rest it needs, we attempt to escape life. Wanting to escape life stems from our illusion that life should be different. We are not willing to accept life as it is. There are many forms of escaping that we can avoid when we slow down and pay attention more closely to life, to the message from our soul.

Eating, Drinking and Resting

Many of us live in noisy cities and lead stressful lives. The stress of life often prevents us from eating healthily and having a restful sleep. Certain habits of food and drink can thwart a restful sleep, such as eating a large and heavy meal close to our bedtime, or drinking alcohol. Alcohol is a diuretic: it forces urination, thus keeping us from sleep. Drinking alcohol can also lead to snoring, which restricts the flow of air in our lungs. This reduces the oxygen in our blood and contributes to a hangover. Coffee, chocolate or cola drinks are better avoided before bedtime, as they contain caffeine. We might also want to abstain before bedtime from foods that contain tyramine. Tyramine can be found in foods such as bacon, cheese, ham, nuts or red wine. It causes the release of norepinephrine, which is a brain stimulant.

Regular exercise helps with our sleeping (but exercise should be avoided shortly before going to bed, as its immediate effect is to stimulate the body). Other sleep aids include lavender oil, herbs, massage, aromatherapy and simple breathing exercises. Regular bedtime and wake-up times help to regulate our body clock, and therefore also help us to sleep more easily.

Overeating

Dennis was a baker. He was heavily overweight and disliked any sort of sport or activity. He also consumed the wrong foods: mostly carbohydrates, sweets and processed food with high levels of salt.

Dennis started to attend several weight-loss groups in his thirties. In the groups, he shared his idea of why he was overeating: high stress levels and feeling depressed with his life. Dennis was a very sensitive person, reacting to situations of injustice and unkindness. He felt that disappointment was a constant companion, and eating provided warm and consistent comfort for him. Dennis also took a high number of aspirins daily, which he felt helped him emotionally.

Dennis confessed that he did not know how to handle his feelings when the going got tough for him. He did not feel very comfortable on a social level either. Sharing his feelings with the groups,

Dennis realised that with his huge body he kept people at bay: his body mass created a physical distance between himself and other people. Fortunately, over time and with the help of being in these groups, Dennis learned to cope with his emotional life more easily. His weight dropped enormously.

There are many physically expressed examples of our emotions and thoughts being out of balance with our soul perspective, for example overeating, anorexia, bulimia, self-cutting or drug abuse. When taking a soul perspective, when our soul is in the driver's seat of all that we are in this life, however, we are constantly nourished. The universe provides nourishment. Yogis have been known to go without food for long times, seemingly relying on spiritual nourishment. While we live a different, less simple and sedate life, we do not have to close ourselves off to this nourishment. We do close ourselves off to it, however, when we ignore the perspective of soul and identify solely with a body-mind perspective. If we fail to acknowledge our spiritual roots, if we ignore our soul perspective, food or other substances can become addictive to us. We can, of course, appreciate and enjoy our food, but more than calories we need to heed the perspective of our soul. Inspiration from our soul is far more nourishing to us than chocolate or alcohol. There is no need to go without the pleasure of good food, but a balanced diet is an expression of a balanced view: we need to eat from a divine perspective.

Soulful Living and Spiritual Discipline

Spiritual Discipline

Without discipline, we allow life, the hectic nature of daily living and the goings-on in the outside world to preoccupy us more than necessary. With a spiritual discipline, we allow ourselves to stay with a soul perspective and lead a more soulful life. A spiritual discipline is individual to us and can have many forms, for example meditation, deep contemplation, or just sitting and being. Our intention and attention can form the cornerstones of a spiritual discipline.

Intention

Without the intention to participate in life to the best of our abilities, we might lose our way. If we lack the intention to have a spiritual discipline, life might just engulf us.

An intention is not a wish, or a 'maybe', or a 'would-be-great'. It is a necessity for action in life. Setting a goal for a spiritual discipline is a start. We can write down this goal and keep it in a visible place for us to see. We can regularly affirm and confirm this goal to ourselves. We can visualise it and make it concrete in our head and heart on a regular basis.

The intent behind our goal clarifies the goal and makes it stronger. Any deliberate and strong intent helps us to shift and co-create our life, and we achieve our goals more easily. This applies to the goal of having a spiritual discipline as well. Our spiritual discipline can become a strong personal urge: we focus on it and want to express it on a regular basis. We expect it to happen, and we make it happen. With this intention, we fix ourselves on a future outcome that is beneficial to us: a permanent perspective of soul, a living from soul, allowing soul to imbue all aspects of who we are. Our personality is softened, we let go of indoctrination from our family, heritage, social class etc., and our ego becomes the expression of soul in this world. Our thinking changes positively, incessant thoughts abate, and our feelings become more and more positive.

We achieve this over time when we have added a spiritual discipline to the fabric of our life. Once our spiritual discipline has become more of a constant variable in our lives, we can and will allow ourselves to choose a perspective of soul more regularly. We have a private audience with the universe, shutting out the distractions of life for a while, and in doing so we refocus on the soul strength that we are.

With a spiritual dimension in our life, we add a dimension of hope and love. When we reflect, contemplate, meditate or just rest and be, or when we walk in nature, call a friend, watch our thinking, slow down or listen to music, we see the world from a perspective of soul and feel love again. With our intention to see life from a soulful perspective, we add that new dimension. Our soul perspective can counteract fearful aspects of life on the outside: unemployment, wars, disasters, human failure and misery. When we look at the world from a perspective of soul, we cease to react with fear to these conditions, but choose only to act with love. We enable ourselves to live life to our fullest potential.

Attention

Our attention keeps us aware of what is happening in our life. This includes the necessity of a spiritual discipline.

When I went shopping today, I saw a young man in a suit leaving the supermarket. Carrying all of his heavy shopping bags in one hand, he was checking his emails on his smartphone with the other. His head was bent; his body and face exuded tension. It was a lovely morning today: the sun was shining and the temperature was mild; a blue sky welcomed us. This man, however, did not notice any of this. He did not seem to see life from a perspective of soul at that moment. A perspective of soul does not mean we do not live in this physical life with all that we encounter. His attention, however, was focussed on his email, and it looked as if he had not experienced the shopping as a positive event. A woman I saw shortly afterwards was rushing along as well. Her gaze was directed at something far away, she felt and looked tense, and she was almost run over by an oncoming car. She did not seem to be paying attention to what was happening around her.

Each moment of our life we make a choice to focus our attention. When we focus on something specific, whatever else is happening around us can often fade into insignificance. When we ignore pain or discomfort in our body, for example (and some people are very good at this), we ignore the physical, mental or emotional changes we need to make to let go of that pain: we do not take the rest that we need when our body is tired or our emotions are shattered. In my experience, pain can be a message we send to ourselves from a soul perspective: a message to pay attention to something we missed. When we pay attention to the message, we can gain insight into the reason for the pain. We can look deeply, change our attitude and often release the pain. If we ignore such messages for a long time, however, the physical reminder can become so strong that we feel unable to let go of pain and dis-ease easily, as it has become too entrenched. It is then that we might become seriously ill.

By paying attention to our discomfort, we might see we are pursuing a detrimental path – today or in general. When we pay attention, we allow our innate wisdom to guide us to let go: our soul reminds us, we remind ourselves, to let go of what hurts and embrace what can heal us. We can connect with love and let go of fear. When seeing life from a soulful perspective, we can notice the benefits of sunshine, or be grateful for the mildness of temperature, or have a realisation of something important. There is joy in this moment. When we do not live consciously from a soulful perspective, we deny life as it is, as it comes to us now.

Most of us are in the midst of life, and our attention needs to be focussed on the outside for a big chunk of the day. We need to pay attention when we cross the street, as we do not want to be run over by a car. We also pay attention at work, because we need to earn a living. Equally, we pay attention to a friend in need, and by so doing we can show and embody friendship, kindness and compassion. We also, however, need to pay attention to our inner life, to the depth of who we are. Our inner life, our soul perspective, is the power that feeds us. We might think we are fed by money, influence, prestige, gossip etc., and indeed these aspects of life might carry us for a while, but for many of us this concept of life will show its flaws eventually: loneliness, a lack of purpose and sense in life, an emptiness, or depression.

The spiritual discipline discussed here is not the discipline of a rigid mind, a discipline that stifles imagination and joy, as we might have experienced as a part of our culture. I felt free of my German indoctrination when I felt I could use my indoctrinated focus and discipline as abilities, to be accessed whenever I needed them. For a long time, I had seen them as shackles preventing me from experiencing joy. A spiritual discipline can be the discipline of gently refocussing on the moment as often as possible, instead of allowing our mind to think incessantly. It can be a gentle and kind observation of our thoughts without judging them.

Over time, with such a discipline, our mind will become more peaceful.

Yes, many of us lead busy lives. Often we allow ourselves to be unaware of our thoughts and do not live from a soulful perspective. However, there are always breaks in our busy lives. We can re-align our attention when we go to the toilet, when we walk through the office, when we fetch a drink, or when we are stretching our body for a moment. Small breaks in our daily routine can become periods of gentle re-focus. We align ourselves with a soulful perspective again when we watch our breathing or use a mantra; such actions instil peace. With time and practice, being present in this moment and seeing life from soul will increasingly become our normal state of being.

Attention to now is a *choice*. Whatever we ignore does, in a sense, not happen to us; though it does technically happen, we choose to screen it out. When we focus our attention internally, we can observe our thoughts and accept them. We can notice which thoughts bring about fear or the absence of joy. With time, when we persist in observing our thoughts, they will change for the positive. We will start living a more soulful life.

Some of us focus on gossip, fear and negative news, as we think we need to be informed. Most of our conversations can seem to be shallow, focussing on these aspects of life. While gossip and world news keep us in touch with the external world, we can also choose to observe and let them pass by, not give them any excessive credit or importance. It is just mind doing what mind is supposed to do: processing external stimuli. We can observe and, at the same time, connect with the love we are inside.

The love we are brings strength to our existence. It serves like a mesh that absorbs external stimuli, the world outside, and infuses it with peace. It brings joy to this moment. In this moment, we are safe, and in the next one. Many moments form an hour, a day, and as they flow from one to the other we experience an existence of joy. From soul, we can look at our internal dialogue, and we can accept and smile at the negativity of it. Once we notice it, are aware of it, we are already in the process of changing it. It might take time, but once we notice and we observe, change is already happening. Trust this.

Our intention and attention are at the centre of our spiritual discipline. Sometimes, however, we are so aware that our body or mind urgently needs healing that we feel that we must achieve this before we are fully able to focus on living from soul. Whenever our body presents us with discomfort, our attention is focussed on dealing with or getting away from this discomfort as quickly as possible. What we fail to realise in this circumstance is, perhaps, that it is our soul that has brought the discomfort or dis-ease to our attention.

Soulful Living and Healing

Healing Our Physical Body

Various reasons can account for physical disease. We might have given our body improper nutrition or neglected physical exercise. Stress in our life takes its toll, and sometimes we have disregarded the signs from our physical body for some time. That can be an inflammation that seems to linger on, a message from our kidneys on and off, a recurrent bladder infection when we have indulged too much, or frequent back problems. There are factors, of course, on which we have a more limited influence: pollutants in the air, water or food. Maybe a genetic disease or disorder was triggered off because of our way of living, feeling or thinking. If we think genetic traits are set in stone, instead of energetic blueprints of our body that can change, we might feel helpless to do anything about our disease.

We still have choices, though. While we have very limited influence on being exposed to pollutants in the air, water and food, we can buy organic food with fewer pollutants and no preservatives. We can eat less and more consciously; eating less can compensate for the higher prices of organic food. We can live more consciously, and doing so will help our body heal itself; we might even avoid a negative genetic trigger leading to disease.

At present, we attempt to heal our world and avoid pollution and deforestation, albeit with limited results. We will all completely clean up our world together one day, though. With billions of people on the Earth, this might take time, but one day there will be a paradigm shift in terms of how we see ourselves: not as separate beings, but as being connected with all that is, being the source and result of all that is. We can already support this change to come by cleaning up our physical body and inner world today. Herbs, vitamins, colonic flushes, specific food items and lots of water free our body of toxins. We can give up smoking and curb our intake of alcohol; we can avoid drugs of any sort, unless we need them to support our healing. When we give our body more rest, or eat more slowly and consciously, we allow our physical body to heal itself.

Soul and body work together. Both communicate with us via, for example, a feeling of dis-ease, or a thought-based reminder, or physical pain, or an intuition. Bodies do not think; they simply work on keeping themselves balanced. Billions of cells work together to create harmony. When we listen to ourselves as soul, when we tune in to our body, we find out what is good for ourselves as a whole. Give your body a chance, and it will heal itself over time.

We can burden our body with our emotions and mind. Perhaps we fail to address old or current emotional wounds: a residue of old grief, or disappointment at a friend's behaviour, or a feeling that we are being abused emotionally by people that we love. Equally, habitual patterns of fearful thinking or a judgmental internal dialogue can affect our physical body. All aspects of ourselves work with and influence each other. If we do not exercise, our mind might become sluggish. A troubled mind might so drain us that we lose the feeling of joy that leads to physical exercise and wellbeing. If we choose to control our emotions with intoxicating substances, our minds cease to be able to think clearly. When we fail to release non-beneficial emotions, or fearful thinking, we place enormous strains on our body.

Healing Our Emotions

Tears and Sadness

Tears and sadness can be invaluable teachers; so often they come bearing important gifts. Some of us might think showing sadness is inappropriate. In our upbringing, we might have been told to suppress emotions, to show a 'stiff upper lip'. Many men find it inappropriate to show emotions in public, and sometimes even in private situations, because they might be seen as a sign of weakness. For others, showing emotion might not fit with a concept of being spiritually enlightened; we might think we 'should' control our emotions with our mind. We might see ourselves as a 'glass-half-full' person and want to avoid emotions we regard as negative. It is perfectly possible, however, to think positively and still acknowledge our 'negative' emotions. We can form a positive life with our thoughts, beliefs and actions, and at the same time emotions can teach us. They can help us with our transformation. We might have forgotten some issues; there might be pain and grief we have not dealt with. It is when we accept and transmute these emotions, and when we go into the depths of them to see their hidden meaning, that we transform our life. We accept life when we accept our emotions. When we learn to be sad, angry or grieving, we accept life and can move forward.

Peter

Peter, a window cleaner, went for an aromatherapy massage session. He suffered from severe back pain. Peter was a highly self-reliant, highly logical person. He had shown tremendous perseverance and stamina throughout his life. The therapist massaging him found that his back muscles were as hard as stones: so hard, in fact, that it was impossible for the treatment to move beneath them into the deeper layers of Peter's back. The hardness prevented any progress beneath the surface, and failed to soften despite six weeks of weekly massage. As the aromatherapist was unable to reduce the tension in Peter's muscles, he remained in severe pain and needed to take strong painkillers.

At his massage sessions, Peter would lie down on the couch and appear keen for progress, but did not seem to be able to relax at all – despite soft music, the gentle scents of the aromatherapy oils, and a loving atmosphere within the room. Jill, the therapist, became convinced that the hardness stemmed from an emotional cause, rather than from hard physical labour, as Peter maintained.

Jill asked Peter how long it had been since he had last felt sadness: since he had last cried. Peter smiled and stated with pride that this had been when he was a very small child. Since then, he had not shed a tear at all. Jill gently suggested to him that this might be part of the reason why he suffered from back pain: he might have stored non-expressed emotions in his body. Peter, however, was unable to accept this as a potential reason for his pain. He was not willing to work with the idea of unexpressed grief, let alone the grief itself. There were a good number of reasons why he could grieve, not least that his parents had died in an accident when he had been 20 years old, and later on his fiancée had left him without warning. It seemed as if Peter had just carried on with his life without giving in to his feelings, even when disaster struck.

Peter went to a different message therapist, and then to another one, after rejecting Jill's suggestions. Her fellow therapists contacted Jill and shared their assessments, and none of them could help Peter at all. He did not want to look beyond the physical level. He decided to continue to use drugs for pain control, instead, and ceased coming for massage.

Many of us will have been in situations where we have felt that we have had to harden ourselves against life. Life has presented challenges, and we have not wanted to give in; we have not wanted to deal with our painful emotions, and might even have felt embarrassed by them in some way. It can also seem sometimes as if the media is full of manmade and natural disasters from across the world, and our immediate response is to want to cocoon ourselves. We might feel that we will break down if we give in to our feelings of fear and vulnerability, that we will be overwhelmed by them, and we also fear that others might perceive us to be weak.

We live in a culture of denial and double standards. Often, those who allow expression of their deepest emotions can be seen as weak, hysterical or immature. At the same time, our emotions can be manipulated on purpose. Look at TV advertising, for example: how often do adverts blatantly manipulate our emotions in order to sell products? Equally, when the television news programmes bring disasters into our living rooms, it is those harrowing images that call on our humanity and move us to donate money. Sometimes, indeed, it can seem that only in such acts of giving money does emotion have any value.

An overexposure to negative news can make us emotionally fatigued, but there is a lesson to be learnt at the same time. We need to accept and work with our emotions, such as grief, anger and envy, as well as joy and exuberance. When we allow ourselves to experience grief, or a sense of loss and pain, we can share our strength of coping when others need our help. Likewise, we can share our positive feelings. Either way, when we block our emotions, it makes it all the harder to express ourselves in the world.

Transforming Emotions

How do we transform those emotions which we regard as disturbing, repetitive and hurtful, without neglecting the learning, the changes that come from them? Pay attention and take responsibility first: name your emotion! Is the drama in your life, your emotional story, disguising the real issue behind the emotion? Sometimes, we might think a certain situation or a specific person's behaviour has caused our outrage, when in fact, with careful reflection, we can see that our outrage comes from a long-held fear. Once we let go of the drama, we can see the real reason. Our drama can overwhelm us. As a first step, we can acknowledge, accept, perhaps even bless our strong emotion. It is telling us a story, revealing a hitherto hidden message.

I remember being very angry in the past. While I thought my current circumstances were responsible, and I felt trapped, over time I realised my anger had a much deeper root. When I allowed myself to pursue this deeper avenue, I allowed a transformation beyond belief. In such an unravelling, we might need professional help; a therapist or counsellor can help us unravel our strong reaction to life and to specific situations.

Sometimes, all we can do is manage our emotion for the time being. A client of mine used to have panic attacks in certain situations. With help, she developed and used a method of jolting herself out of the emotion into which she was thrown when these trigger situations occurred. Once she had learnt to do that, she felt calm enough to look the emotion in the face. With time, she turned her life around.

Do not allow your emotions to overwhelm you! Breathe deeply when a strong emotion threatens to overcome you, find a quiet spot, remove yourself from the situation and centre yourself. Doing so will lower your heartbeat and blood pressure, which in itself will soften your 'negative' emotion straight away. When we see ourselves as a coherent being, we accept that emotions and mind work together, that our emotional health is connected with our mental health; we transform our emotions with the help of our mind.

Healing Our Mind

We have a number of tools to hand that we can use to transform our strong emotions. Our mind can analyse the situation to find the reason behind the strong emotion. Is the emotion coming from an entrenched and unhelpful underlying belief? We might, for example, have been told in our childhood that we lacked social grace, and so as adults we experience feelings of panic each time we are in a crowd. We have come to believe we are not good at social situations. Equally, perhaps we might have been told as children that the world is an unsafe place and that we have to compete against others to survive. Accordingly, as adults our competitiveness brings up anger and strong disappointment whenever we are not the centre of attention.

With emotional habits like these, choosing a more empowering belief can help. A first step can be an immediate choice for love, instead of the fear inherent in the negative emotion. This can be done through a mantra, like 'I choose love'. We can connect with love by slowing down our breathing, and breathing into our heart space. By doing this, we let go of fear at the very moment of experiencing it. Next, we can look into the reason for the strong emotion, analyse it, work with the situation and change our future responses to similar situations over time. Unhelpful emotions serve a purpose: they show us how we have identified with fear. Once we let go of resistance to the emotion and choose to work with it from a perspective of love, we can transmute the fear.

Our emotional wellbeing contributes to our overall health. Emotional wellbeing means being able to express our emotions and to learn about and from them. When we have emotional wellbeing, we are resilient and able to cope with our emotions, to influence our emotions and to have meaningful social interactions. Emotional health is a personal concept and has different meanings for all of us. Some of us have varying degrees of what we call 'emotional intelligence'. Others are more mind-driven and have a stronger cap on their emotions. None of these approaches is better or worse; they are just different. Our individual makeup is perfect for our story of life, and serves us on our journey.

The journey of life allows us to change. Maybe we want to become more emotionally aware, and we have the choice to work on that. On the other hand, our strong emotions might get us into trouble, and we might struggle to cope with them. Our mind can help us to control, shift or transmute such emotions. Attention to our thoughts, to our internal dialogue, helps with change; it shows us how certain (often negative) thoughts can influence our emotions. Mind techniques such as breathing, slowing down, contemplation, reflection and especially meditation can help us to achieve a clearer, more positive mind. With time, we can adjust and smooth our personality, soften our emotions, and liberate our thinking processes, moving them beyond the rigidity of ingrained patterns. All that is needed is a willingness, and the patience, to use our mind to explore our emotions and thinking in a peaceful and relaxed manner. With time taken to pay attention to our reactions to life and to the mirror we see in others and their reactions to us, we provide the framework for change.

Our emotional health is strongly connected with our mental health. Emotional good health means that we can cope with life events, and that we can acknowledge and respect emotions within ourselves and in others. Our emotional health is shaped by life, and sometimes when we experience difficulty it can be hard to hold onto our emotional health.

As a coherent being, we cannot separate our mind from our body either. Mental health can be affected by our physical health and vice versa. My grandfather was in constant physical pain in the last years of his life and was habitually ill-tempered because of it. Equally, mentally stressed people are irritable, their bodies are tense and they are consequently plagued by tension headaches. As stated earlier, if our mental faculties are impaired, through physical illness, perhaps, or through taking recreational drugs such as alcohol, we might struggle to see obvious danger such as traffic approaching at speed when we are crossing a busy road, and we can hurt ourselves more easily. Sometimes grief, too, has a profound physical effect: deep lines appear on our face, our body seems subdued, and we do not stand upright any more, as if the grief is weighing heavily on our upper body.

Our conscious mind filters every thought, feeling and experience. It judges, compares and accepts or rejects data from outside sources. All our past feelings and experiences are stored in our subconscious mind. We would be overwhelmed if we were conscious of all the feelings, thoughts and experiences in our life right now. Our subconscious is our guardian and protector. Both conscious and subconscious mind, however, can hinder healing and positive change. Let us look again at the consequences of absorbing misleading information, thoughts or beliefs in the past. If, as children, we were repeatedly told that the world is an unsafe place, as adults we might want to stay with an unsatisfactory job or situation, as we fear the consequences of change. We might not even want to connect with more positive thoughts, as we fear disappointment, and so we play it safe.

Our mind is the architect of our experiences in the outer and inner world. We create our own reality. A deep healing of the mind – a health-giving alteration to our perspective on life – is not always a quick or easy process. Our world has witnessed some miracle healings, but we do not know how they have happened. I remember witnessing a healing process by an Israeli healer many years ago. A wheelchair-bound woman entered the room for healing. She had not been able to walk for many years, yet when she left the room after the healing session she was able to take her first tentative steps into a new life. Was this healing purely physical – a miracle granted to her from the outside – or did her belief about her ability to walk change? Healing, whether of our body, emotions or mind, is often a result of a transformation: a letting go of living from fear in its various forms. We let go of fear and its many expressions: envy, anger, jealousy etc., and embrace love and its many expressions: acceptance, joy, compassion and trust. Gaining a perspective of love is a process, and at first we may stay with it only occasionally, but as we practise and develop we will stay with it more and more often. Step by step we begin to re-discover our deeper nature: the love that we are.

As we allow ourselves to become aware of what our mind builds internally from our experiences in the external world, we begin to live a more soulful life. When we watch our thoughts and how they affect our actions, when we question our unhelpful beliefs and attitudes, we minimise continuation of the destructive patterns and situations in our lives. Using our example of being brought up to believe that the world is unsafe: we can choose to let go of such a fear and to connect with the love within us instead. We can recall situations where we have felt safe (we will all have had these) and when our courage to go beyond our usual behaviour was strong. Positive-experience anchoring techniques such as this are very useful tools. With time and practice, our life will change, and that change begins as soon as we are willing to pay attention to our thoughts and feelings. With each step we take, we practise living from soul.

Old patterns might lie hidden beneath the radar of our awareness. We might be aware of only a tiny piece of them. Negative, frightening experiences from childhood could be well hidden, although their influence may be powerful enough to force us to recreate inner dramas until we begin to pay attention to our internal dialogue. When we do pay attention, we might very well discover our inner judge. S/he sees life through the prism of our prior experiences. If we experienced rejection and a lack of love in childhood, we will grow up believing that we cannot be loved the way we are, and we will be stuck in childhood behaviour, behaving in ways that make us the centre of attention; attention for bad behaviour is still better than no attention at all. When we are filled with fear, we judge everything from a basis of fear. It paralyses us; we cannot move forward.

Our inner critic is a companion to our inner judge. We might not consciously hear our inner critic, but that will not stop us from reacting to our critic's echoing of real and perceived criticism in our life. Our reactions to the world are largely coloured by our internal criticisms about ourselves.

Most of us, however, felt joy as a child. This joyful child is still within us, and we yearn for joy; we want to play, to create our life. Our inner judge and critic might have silenced our inner child, and our past experiences, our negative thought patterns and the fear hidden in our suppressed emotions might have wounded our inner child, but s/he can start to come out and play again.

By paying attention, we can slowly begin to release our childhood joy again. By living from soul, we can begin to confirm the love that we are again. We can use tools such as therapy and healing, affirmations and visualisations, contemplation and meditation to help us to live more and more from soul. Our attention in every moment shows us we are safe. Our past can be seen with compassion, and past misdeeds seem less harsh. We can let go of judgment and temper our emotions. When we pay attention, we gain understanding of our inner world, and of how our inner world is shaped by our outer world, and that understanding will lead to change.

We do not have to listen to our inner critic and judge; they are simply voices. We might have to accept that our childhood and experiences in society have taught us to repress and distort our own emotional process in order to survive in a frightening world. We might have to accept that they have taught us to be emotionally dishonest with ourselves. When we go within, however, we discover a source of unconditional love. Through our meditation, rest or contemplation, when we practise simply being, we can re-access a sense of wisdom and power; we can see ourselves and the world from soul again. Our old patterns can be healed over time. When our inner critic or judge starts speaking, we can shift our perspective there and then.

Our judge and critic are manifestations of fear. As we pay attention, we will come across emotions we were not aware of, because they lie deeply buried within our subconscious. Once we honour their presence, we can see where healing is needed. Uncomfortable as this might be, if we stick with the process of observation and exploration, we will heal ourselves with time.

When we see our lives and ourselves from the perspective of soul, from a higher vantage point, we can develop new, more helpful beliefs. We can release old traumatic emotions and experiences, perhaps with the help of therapy, and we can create a new sense of being. Old thinking patterns will die away and we will begin to feel ourselves more of a creator than a victim of life. Joy and inner peace will accompany our healing.

Soul Communication – Healing and Health

Soulful living means we are willing to be sensitive to and to listen to the messages from our soul. Our soul does not have a voice as such, but speaks through the other elements of our coherent being: our mind, emotions and physical body. Given the complexity of our existence, there are many means of soul communication. We can receive communication through symbols and dreams, intuition, sudden impulses, an unexpected thought or inspiration, or a specific feeling that does not go away. Our bodies, minds and emotions form both the vehicle through which our soul communicates with us, and the vehicle through which our soul experiences life.

Examples of soul messages can include a sudden onslaught of illness through which our soul communicates that we are in an unsustainable pattern of self-neglect. This message is a reminder to look at the obvious, to pay attention. Alternatively, we might burst into tears repeatedly, or frequently lash out in anger. We need to pay attention to these messages of dis-ease too. Equally, if we suffer from migraines, perhaps it is a soul message that our incessant thoughts are overburdening our mind to such an extent that they are affecting our body. The message of the migraines is to let go, relax and soften our mind. For all soul messages, we need to look at the clues that life provides and respond to them by working out the source of the dis-ease.

Perhaps some of us are scared of our feelings because we are afraid that, if we express them, they will reveal too much about us. Our feelings might confuse us, and, if so, we need to slow down to look at them and analyse them with our mind. Our feelings, however, also allow us to explore ourselves, although it is wise to avoid the confusion and dis-ease that can arise from an over-identification with our feelings, and equally wise to avoid basing our decisions solely on the way that we feel. We are not our feelings. Our soul communicates via our emotions and mind, and if we want to change our life, we need to listen to the wholeness that we are. Our mind, including our rational, logical, objective thought processes, can figure out the impulses from our soul; our mind can lead, and our feelings can follow. Our mind helps us to examine external situations objectively. Our feelings are more subjective, expressing internal reflections, but they are also, indeed, a response to life and to the situations within which we find ourselves, and as such they provide valuable clues for the mind. Both thought and emotion are tools for discernment that ideally work in harmony together; neither is better or worse than the other.

Like the multi-faceted, coherent beings that we are, life is a story with many aspects. We are meant to live within and express the wholeness/coherence that we are. Spirit, soul, thoughts, emotions, ego and personality all form this wholeness that we are in this life. Sometimes, it is our mind that gives directions. At other times, our emotions stop us in our tracks, forcing us to pay attention. Our personality might need fine-tuning: subtle changes to smooth our encounters with others. There will be times when our ego needs to push us forward, as we would otherwise hesitate and let an opportunity fade away. Equally, there will be times when we might receive a very strong feeling, a soul impulse, to wait and not to push ahead: a message that it is time to take stock, not to rush, as we might injure ourselves, or run around in a vicious circle, or make a decision that could be a repetition of an old pattern.

Mind-Body-Emotion

We are what we think. Our thoughts are recorded in every cell of our body, whether they stem from inner reflections or they are reactions to external events. We are wholeness, as all aspects of who we are form a holistic whole. Each cell in our body shares the intelligence of the whole. When we change the way we think, we change the energy in our body.

In our society, disease seems to have been accepted as a way of life, and people can come to identify with their disease very closely. Patients talk of 'my cancer', 'my depression' etc. The disease seems to provide a focus, a meaning, an identification with a specific part of life.

This identification with the disease might not be intentional, but might instead arise because patients experience love, care and attention from others when the illness occurs. Some people take a very long time to recover from their illness, and some never recover. Perhaps the process of healing is delayed or suspended in these instances because the attention that the patients receive is so important. In the attention, care and focus from other people that illness brings, especially to patients who feel neglected or who are terribly lonely, illness can provide what is called a 'secondary gain': the gain of love, attention and focus. We are each responsible for giving attention to ourselves, but sometimes we feel unable to do this, and need and crave the attention of others. Such attention fills a void in our life. We might be so scared of losing that attention, of returning to the void, that our healing process might be delayed.

Martha

Martha was a woman deeply unhappy in her marriage. Her husband, Jack, was habitually cold and unable to show his emotions. For him, what Martha regarded as the precious act of communion called 'making love' was nothing more than 'sex': the relieving of a purely biological urge. Jack was not able to show tenderness. A poorly educated labourer, he had worked very hard throughout his adult life, and all that he wanted to do during the remainder of his working life and after retiring was rest, read the paper, watch television and go to the pub. Football was his hobby, and he loved to watch it. Martha, on the other hand, yearned to travel, to learn new things, and to communicate avidly with her husband and other people. Martha also loved to be in nature, and hated being inside the house most of the time.

Martha and Jack had raised two children, both of whom had left home early on, as they had wanted to find and live a different kind of life, and both of whom had achieved success in their own career. Neither liked to visit their parents too often, because of the constant quarrelling between them. Martha felt a deep void in her life, but even if her husband had been able to listen patiently, she would not have been able to voice her emotions.

Martha had been one of seven siblings, and her early marriage to Jack had seemed a wonderful escape from her surroundings. Coming from such a large family, Martha had also experienced very little love from her parents during her childhood, and she had desperately hoped to find strong love in her marriage. Martha had not learnt a profession, nor had she ever gone out to work during her married life. Her work had centred on caring for Jack, the children and the family home.

Shortly after the children left home, Martha became ill with sickening headaches and painful menstrual problems. Jack was unable to cope with her illness, and simply dismissed it for a few years.

Eventually, however, Martha developed Parkinson's disease, and Jack could no longer ignore the illness. He was faced with the stark choice of either admitting his wife to a nursing home or looking after her himself. Given Jack's strong sense of duty, he decided to look after Martha in their home. He felt the burden of looking after her, but he did his very best to do so.

After a while, he and Martha began to talk to each other more and more. They started to communicate in a way that they had never achieved before. In the course of looking after his wife, Jack also began to express his considerable capacity for compassion. During the seven years that he looked after Martha, Jack underwent a slow but powerful transformation. He developed more tenderness, and Martha received from him a degree of love and attention that she had hardly experienced before. Her illness seemed to fill a void in her life, and, equally, her illness gave Jack a renewed sense of purpose. Jack looked after Martha until the last day of her life. To this day, he speaks very fondly of Martha, and is clearly a man at peace with himself.

Disease

Mankind is afflicted with many diseases, stemming from many different sources, such as viruses, bacteria, parasites and toxins. Long years of physical abuse, excessive drug intake or severe depression can also take their toll. Other factors can include malnutrition, exposure to extreme climates or harsh, punishing work, prolonged emotional distress, genetic susceptibility etc. There are so many possible combinations of causal factors that it can be difficult to unravel and identify each of the threads that have contributed to the manifestation of the disease.

Disease, however, can also be a belief, a label we attach to our condition. This label can keep the condition in place, preventing us from seeing the disease as a temporary imbalance. Any imbalance in our life, in our body, can be an opportunity, a reminder to redirect our life. It can be a reminder to replace outdated thoughts and beliefs that are holding us back, to let go of detrimental habits or fears, or to abandon old stuck emotions such as grief. Once we let go of these, healthier options will take their place.

When we invite a change into our life, such as the healing of illness, we are asked to let go of old, toxic energy and welcome the process of healing. We do not need to know the full process of this letting go; we merely need to take the first step. This can be our willingness to change, despite feeling anxious about it. The next step will appear, another one will occur to us, the following one might come via a friend or a book, and an event might bring change in us or in our circumstances. If we trust the process of life, it will not let us down.

When we treat disease superficially, we only disguise the issue. Drugs help us remove the symptoms, but can they heal the causes? Yes, if we talk about a bacterial infection, perhaps, but what healing can drugs give to the reasons causing us to abuse our body, or to hold on to emotional trauma, or to feel we need secondary gains such as attention through illness? We might feel righteous, for example, when we hold on to thoughts of superiority that seem to provide us with strength, but we also lessen our ability to experience and express compassion and peace.

We can be tempted to blame our physical environment for our disease, or the limits we took on board with our cultural or social heritage. We can blame our upbringing, the pain inflicted by our parents, our personality or our genetic makeup, which seemingly cannot be changed.

A toxic environment, however, might be a result of toxic thinking, feelings, habits and beliefs: a thinking pattern that clings to the superficial security of our social and cultural heritage, or the self-abuse that makes us feel alive. Extreme feelings, outbursts of anger can provide a semblance of control and importance. Equally, we can cling to a religious or other belief that keeps us deeply entrenched in fear: a fear that is connected to a feeling of spiritual superiority and being different, important. All this is our choice. If we think we do not have a choice in this, we automatically define ourselves as victims. We do not have much choice as a victim; the (often subconscious) choice to regard ourselves as a victim reduces our choices for change. We might lack the understanding and tools for change right now, but this will not always be the case. We always have choice.

Choice is our willingness for change, even though we might not know in this moment how to change. When we decide to change, change will come: with the wish to change our beliefs with time, and with different thoughts, or new friends, or newly discovered tools for change. In my experience, a soul reminder to move forward and grow is often behind change. A sudden urge to live a different life, the feeling of being fed up with our situation, a friend giving us an honest assessment of ourselves: these are all clues from a soul perspective. While our soul is the instigator of change, our ego can be the agent, aligned to our soul, taking action, propelling us forward. When we change our toxic thinking, we start cleansing both our cells and our lifestyle. When we accept responsibility for our health, this happens on many levels: eating more healthy food, observing our emotional wellbeing, working with our toxic thoughts. We can slow down our life and pay more attention; we can allow ourselves time for change. Perhaps we can change country or job, decide on a less hectic or superficial lifestyle, choose to embrace nature and our stillness within. Doing any of this will move us towards greater health.

Sometimes, as previously mentioned, we might want to use a therapeutic method to heal ourselves. As every reader will be aware, there are many valid forms of therapy and healing. In this book, I would like to focus on music, because it is a form of healing which, in my experience, has often been underestimated. Here are just a few words about music as a healer.

Music Is a Great Healer

Friends who play music tell me that when doing so they are in a different world. They seem to feel as if their music captures them and brings to the fore their inner life, their thoughts and feelings, and above all their soul.

Music seems to lift the soul, change our emotions and allow us, for a moment, to let go of life's turmoil. When singing together, or playing an instrument in a group, we can connect with the feeling of common goals and understanding. When we connect with a group of likeminded people in this way, we lift their souls with our contribution and vice versa; all together are creative, and, by focussing their emotions and thoughts on the musical practice, all are being in the moment, all are present. A group of souls creates, and all are lifted in the process: both those creating and those listening to the music. At the moment we connect our inner self with a group to create music, and we pay attention to the energy of the music being created, we are lifted from sorrow, and our soul is lifted, even if only for that moment.

Music allows us to go within, to pay attention to our feelings. It inspires and consoles us and, at that moment of listening, enables us to let go of our current life. When we hear ourselves creating or listening to music, we hear the note of our soul. This note can expand; we expand, and we go beyond our current boundaries. We learn to pay attention and to connect with the joy within us, despite sorrow; we connect with, experience and expand our inner world. Music is beauty, the beauty of sound, and its richness provides hope and opens our heart and our senses. Throughout history, enslaved peoples have sung together to lift their souls when working in the fields. In Ireland, fishermen would sing together to overcome their fears and connect with the divine when their vessels were being tossed about in high seas. Singing is beneficial for our soul and mind. Music seems to be able to unblock our thinking; it helps us to have clearer dreams, relax deeply and develop trust in life. The joy behind our singing is an expression of our connection to life.

Music has been known as a channel for healing for a long time. In ancient Greece, certain modes of music were regarded as having a great influence on our emotions. Can you imagine a great film without powerful music in it? Music enhances the mood of a film and deepens the audience's connection to the film's unfolding story. We often remember certain songs we heard in a film. The music helps us to understand emotionally what we are being shown.

Music appeals to our emotions, and playing music together connects us together. Playing music, singing gives the feeling of creative achievement. Musical therapy helps patients to find balance in their emotions and soul again. When we sing or play an instrument, we express our feelings, and in doing so we connect with ourselves, with our soul. Even when we only passively listen to music, it can calm us, restore our balance. Music is a wonderful agent for healing.

Music can help us to overcome fear and obstacles, to create joy, to connect with the joy within us and to restore enthusiasm. It nourishes and strengthens our soul. Music can also stimulate our imagination, creating pictures and scenarios within us that help us to understand how we can live, develop and be free. Music can release emotional blockages, freeing trapped energy and so helping us to move forward in life. Let music be the agent for connecting with your deeper self on a regular basis, either by listening to music or by singing and/or playing an instrument. Music is one of many resources we can use to link with our soul. It enables us to leave our hectic life behind for a while, and to strengthen the link with our soul.

Soulful Living in the Practice of Life II

Our Past Does Not Define Us

Whatever we have done in the past, it does not need to define us. Perhaps we have shown the darker aspects of ourselves, our shadow side: violence, rage, jealousy, greed or envy. Such expressions might have led to feelings of guilt, and, while guilt pushes us to take a close look at ourselves and our behaviour, it can also hold us back in life. When guilt leads to introspection and consequent change, however, it has served a benign purpose. Having felt guilty can prevent us from embodying our darker side in the future, or maybe the next time we slip will be in a less severe way. The act of slipping can also act as a reminder: a reminder to watch our shadow side, so we have a better chance of making a different, more soulful choice next time.

Guilt can be a prison cell, if we are not able to let it go. Our past behaviour, the mistakes we have made: these do not need to define the rest of our lives, unless we choose to remain stuck within them. The prospect of a better future can define our lives instead. We can all connect with hope for a better future ahead. We define our future by our present actions, by our attitude towards life, by our insights and the promise of change we make to ourselves, by our understanding that change is a process. The process of our past has enabled us to become who we are now, and the choices for change that we make now will define our future.

Life defines us, and living life shapes us. Living life with passion entails making 'mistakes', even severe ones. Feedback from what we regard as 'mistakes' helps us to move forward. If we allow ourselves to be scared of making mistakes, we can refuse to live life with passion. Avoiding 'the feedback of life' takes away experience, and it is experience that leads to change. We can avoid some 'mistakes' by introspection, by observing life and others, but, if we are willing to look at the feedback of life without prejudice, it enables us to go within, to look at who we are and at who we want to become. When we have hurt someone we respect and love, for example, we might feel guilty about it. When we find compassion for ourselves at that moment, however, we can open ourselves up to a deeper understanding; we can learn, for example, that it is possible for us to hurt someone without any intention to do so at all. Realising this, we can determine to think more clearly next time before we talk and act. We can also realise that, ultimately, we are not responsible for the feelings others have; only they are, and we can accept that what we said was said with the best of intentions. In all learning, we see deeper, we widen our vista and we live more from the wisdom of soul.

The prospect of a better future, of a better version of ourselves, can encourage us to live life with passion. From a soulful perspective there is no judgment. When we live from soul, we can allow the 'feedback of life' to inform our future behaviour gently.

We cause change to come about by working with the 'feedback of life', by allowing what we call 'mistakes'. Without 'mistakes' we cannot achieve a better version of ourselves. It is not the past that defines us (although we can learn from it) but what we do with the 'feedback' from it; we define and model ourselves by determining what we choose to become. What we do not express at this moment in time, for example compassion, non-judgment, passion or acceptance, can become part of our makeup ten, 20 or 30 years ahead. Our past reminds and teaches us, the future is our hope, but it is the present that always defines us. The 'now' is the testing ground for a different version of ourselves: the one that comes to us from the perspective of soul.

Past Present Future

Look to this day,
For it is life,
The very life of life,
In its brief course lies all
The realities and verities of existence,
The bliss of growth,
The splendour of action,
The glory of power,
For yesterday was a dream,
And tomorrow is only a vision.
But today, well lived,
Makes every yesterday a dream of happiness
And every tomorrow a vision of hope.
Look well, therefore, to this day.
Sanskrit proverb

Time is a concept that allows us to deal with space. We are not really living in time; we are living in space (mind space). We move through the space of our life, not through the time span. The time span is just a concept to measure the space in which our life is experienced.

Time helps us to structure our experiences in life. When it comes to our experience of time, however, there is only ever a never-ending process of now. The now is also only a moment. Once we notice and pay attention to the now, it has already gone; it has become the past.

While our concept of time is illusionary, we can still work with it. From a soul perspective, our past is a memory, but we can learn from it. The future never happens, as the future of tomorrow is the reality of today once tomorrow arrives, but the future can offer hope. We learn from the past, take action in the now and project hope into the future. Our concept of time places events that happen to us into a context of the evolving self.

How does knowing this help us to take a soulful perspective more often? From a soulful perspective, we can choose the now more often: to make the present count, to let go of the past and to trust in the future. We can choose to trust in the unfolding process of life, and that it will bring to us whatever is needed. Being in the now means enjoying life more fully, freeing ourselves from the shackles of past guilt or fear for the future. We engage more fully with whatever is happening in the present moment. Past experiences offer learning to the present, and our present understanding feeds into our future plans; all become part of the continuum of experience.

Experience has to be lived before it can be used to inform our choices about how we live now. The results of each choice will inform our future choices about living. There is no need to dwell on (live in) the past and future if we accept that in the present we are calling on our learning from the past and on our plans for the future. The continuum of life is rather like taking a train journey: we boarded at one station, are now several stations down the line and have yet to reach our destination. What is important is experiencing where we are now. We would not be there without the boarding station or the destination; they inform the now. Our past feeds back to us what we might change or do again, and the promise of what our future holds keeps us steady: it is the motivation behind the engine. What matters is allowing ourselves to fully experience where we are, because by the next station it will be gone and the opportunity to live in that now will have passed.

When we spend time worrying about or regretting what happened in the past and being afraid of what might happen tomorrow, we cannot enjoy life now. If we are focussed on our worry, we do not notice what is happening now. Worrying about the past keeps us in bondage to it. Sometimes, we hold on to the past because it is familiar, but being in the past is being with the dead, is like living on a burial ground. When we live in the past, memories and unfinished business control our emotional wellbeing.

When we are stuck in the past or the future, we are stuck in the ego-mind and cannot live from soul.

Our past, of course, has helped us to become who we are. We treasure important memories, and there will be situations that motivate us to revisit our past in order to learn and change for the now. Our past can give us important lessons; whether on a personal or societal level, we can learn from the past to create a better future.

The future offers us hope. Our present situation can be difficult to accept; we suffer. Seeing our future as more positive can help us cope with the present. All of us will experience difficult periods in life when we are presented with deep challenges: a loss of something or someone, for example, or financial difficulties, war or hunger. We might also encounter a shadow side of ourselves with which we need to work, and to which we cannot find a solution in the present moment.

We might want to control our life, make it safe and secure. At the same time, we are afraid of what the future might bring, like losing our job, the people we love or our possessions. We try to control our future, and we wait for the moment in which we believe that everything will be as we want it to be, but this moment can never arrive; life is only ever available now. When we run away from the now, we are not in contact with our soul; we are neither living from nor expressing it. We lack spontaneous joy and the peace of seeing life from soul.

When we do see life from soul, we are able to let go of the past, we can stop running away from the now and start living in it, and by so doing we can bring into creation a positive future. We also feel a profound internal peace. Are we not exactly where we need to be right here and now? When looking from the perspective of soul, we are expressing exactly what is needed just now. Nothing needs to be changed. Our individual story in life is unique and offers exactly what we need to become more of who we are, to be more aware. Once we know and accept this, we liberate ourselves, and that is soulful living. In this, we do not have to solely hope for future improvements, and there is no need for transformation either. There is no need for a still mind, an egoless state. Life is now; we can take a soulful perspective now.

Some factors can hold us back from living a more conscious life. They can desperately remind us of the need for change. They urge us to let go, move on and arrive here, instead of staying with the past or the future. These factors are different for all of us: guilt, grief, an addiction to gossip, anger, envy, bitterness, judgment, intolerance, fear for the future, self-righteousness about our past or future direction, and many more. Most of us will have identified with some of these, and that is okay. Let them be a reminder to us to strive for change and improvement. We might have to work through them, but eventually we will move past them; we will let them go because we will cease to need to live in the fear and confusion that engenders them. Having moved beyond them, we will realise that there never was a need to identify with any of them, and we can bless them and focus on the now.

Our Internal and External Worlds

We have all the resources, the energy and wisdom to lead a balanced life in the now without fear. When we see life from the inner perspective of soul, we are in touch with the energy of love that we are. We can experience this love when we deeply contemplate or meditate, when we give or receive healing, when we pray or sing, when we read uplifting books, when we relax with candle light or walk in nature. When we make a choice to see our world from soul, we might have sudden insights, epiphanies. An event, a friendship or our compassion for the plight of others might shift our awareness of life towards a soulful one. Sometimes, when we awake from restful sleep, there can be a moment of connection to our deeper internal world of soul that makes us struggle to connect to the external for a little while. These moments of transition into a different perspective, which can also occur when we are drifting into sleep, allow a stronger connection to our inner world.

On the other hand, the external world can present us with fear-based thoughts and emotions. We might lead stressful lives, rushing from one appointment to the next. We use our mobile phones incessantly to text, talk, email, Twitter etc. At work, we are often bullied, and pressure is piled on us to perform at our best each day, while the threat of redundancy is a constant companion. We spend our evenings watching violent, suspenseful programmes on TV. We might connect to the drama of work, friends, celebrity stories, war and poverty. We might feel that our future is uncertain and dangerous, and that crime, drug abuse and violence are on the increase. Perhaps we feel depressed, dragging ourselves through the working week and living only for the weekend and the holidays. Our life might lack peace and joy, and we might fear for the future. When we over-identify with our external drama, fear can creep into our lives and we feel powerless. When this happens, we need to slow down, breathe deeply and re-affirm our perspective of soul again – and we can shift our perspective in that moment.

John

Since joining a prestigious investment bank straight after graduation, John had led an interesting, but highly stressful, life. He was at the top of his game within the bank for a number of years. In his late twenties, he had a state-of-the-art flat in one of the most exclusive areas of London. He liked fast cars and long nights in the bar to celebrate big deals. With many casual relationships with beautiful women, a fast-paced life at the weekends and frequent superb holidays in beauty spots around the world, John thought that he had it all. In his early thirties, he was the envy of his colleagues. He loved his job; he was the first one in, the last one out, and his bonus cheque was the biggest among his peers. He enjoyed the adrenaline rush of a big deal on the stock exchange, the exhilaration of being the first one to spot an opportunity, the anxiety of waiting to find out whether it was working out and the endorphin release when he realised that he had won the game.

By his late thirties John was made director of his department. About the same time, however, he visited his doctor for a routine check-up and was advised very seriously to slow down and take life more easily, as he was on the brink of burnout. While John understood that in theory this could happen, he dismissed it. Why would it happen to him, when he was so much more resilient than most people?

A few months later, though, John exploded when a deal that one of his team members had initiated collapsed. The vice president of the company to which John reported held John entirely responsible for the deal's failure, and placed enormous pressure on him to rectify the situation by compensating for the lost deal. John immediately began to feel as if a huge weight were lying on his heart, and his heart began to palpitate furiously. He knew that he was dangerously near to a heart attack. A few days later, he was rushed to hospital and his suspicion was confirmed. He had to stay in hospital for a few weeks, and was prescribed drugs to stabilise his condition and mood.

Confined to his flat to recuperate, John felt like a failure. He felt useless and depressed. A friend recommended that he take part in a group of fellow sufferers who had experienced high stress leading to subsequent health problems.

Over the coming months, John learnt through the group a number of techniques for relaxation. He slowly began to shift his view of life towards a more joyful and peaceful one. After a year, he accepted a much less stressful but still pleasingly challenging job.

When John was confronted by fear, anxiety and stress in the new job, he immediately applied one of the techniques that he had learnt in the group. One day, a colleague put pressure on him to accomplish a task, and John could feel the fear that his colleague was experiencing. He had the feeling this fear was going to find a place in his own heart, where it would nest and stay, causing indigestion and pressure. John went for a short break outside and sat down on a bench. Sitting there, he used his breathing to calm his nerves and body. He then visualised love and strength in his heart centre, and made a deliberate choice for a soulful, loving perspective from this powerful internal place of peace and joy. John imagined an orb in his heart filled with different colours: red for strength, blue for peace, green and pink for joy and love. He visualised these colours radiating throughout his body, spreading outwards. As he did so, he saw all grey and darker colours moving away from his body. Within a few minutes John felt refreshed. Coming back into the office, he was able to smile at his colleague and work with peace and joy.

Looking back at his life, John came to realise that his pressurised job, heart attack and ensuing depression had all helped him to see life from a deeper perspective of soul. He was still competitive and realistic, and very much down to earth. At the same time, the events in his external life had brought him to a point that allowed him to feel compassion for others. In essence, he had come to live from a soulful perspective while still functioning fully in the external world. He had learnt to live a more balanced life.

The Power of Difficult Choices

Sometimes life deals us cards that can threaten our ability to cope, which can leave us feeling as if they have shattered us into a thousand pieces. A marriage break-up, a bereavement, losing one's job, the realisation of the loss of youth, bankruptcy, a disaster: these are events that can make us feel helpless and lost, that leave us unable to find a way out. All we can do in these situations is be with life, accept it, without reaching to understand why life has dealt us such a blow. It might look as if life has brought us to a point where we face only extremely tough choices. Often, however, it is exactly at this point that we are about to make an enormous breakthrough in our experience of who we are.

Tough choices can mean that we ask ourselves to jump forward from a perspective of soul. They come at the right time. Deep down, while our minds are deliberating a way forward, we can sense this. We might feel that we cannot make a choice, as any available choice seems too tough. In a situation like this, the only choice we might have is to embrace the situation, stay with it, as tough as it seems. Life, our soul, has brought this situation into our lives, and our ego and personality simply need to catch up. This is a time to simply be, to create space for thinking, to allow ourselves to sit with emotions of discomfort rather than running away from them. We can align all aspects of who we are with the greater purpose of soul. Our choices are not difficult at all; they are just crucial to our progress. We arrive at such choices only a few times in our life. They arrive at critical junctures.

These moments present us with an opportunity to remember who we really are. We are a divine being living through our body-mind, and, at these difficult times, life and our soul are inviting us to remember this. Life is not about right or wrong, and we can abstain from judging our thoughts, emotions and actions. Each juncture simply invites us to deeply refocus on who we are: soul holding together body, mind and emotions. We might choose to work with a more focussed spiritual discipline at these times, with clear attention and intention. The difficult situation within which we find ourselves particularly encourages this, but we always have a choice to do it: to see life and ourselves from a perspective of soul at any time through meditation, contemplation or just being. Life can be hectic, and we tend to slip in our discipline. Fortunately, life will always remind us to see the events in our lives from the perspective of soul. Life always asks us to bring our life, our personality and ego, all we have come to be in our life, into alignment with our greater soul purpose. This purpose might be a grand, special plan, but for many of us it might simply mean simplifying our life, living with purpose, in whatever role or function that might entail.

When, through intention and attention, we regularly align ourselves with soul, we will shift our perspective. This in itself is purpose enough, because, by so doing, we will experience and live from the love, compassion, peace and joy that form the core of who we are: our soul. We can do this now, today, tomorrow, the day after, often. It can become part of our process of life. Life will always respond and bring about the task ahead.

Life and our soul allow us to serve in many ways. Serving the purpose of soul can mean simple acts of compassion, a smile for a stranger, lending a sympathetic ear or abstaining from a judgment. It can be becoming aware of our fears, working with them and letting them go. Every experience is an opportunity to serve; all are welcome, all are important, and, as we serve, the illusory importance of fame, power and prestige will fall away. We serve in simplicity and peace. This way, we also return to the simple joy and delight in the world, and in every moment, that we knew as children. Life will present the next step. Our self-awareness, feelings and searching will help us, always, to address what lies ahead. At the same time, we can quietly observe, watch life unfold, and see our next step presenting itself.

Sometimes, life can seem to be a dream. When we react to it solely with our body-mind and ego, we ignore a soulful perspective, and fear forms the basis of our decisions and reactions. We react from a set of conditioned belief systems. When we wake up from this dream, either suddenly or gradually, and begin living from soul, we remember completely who we are.

For most of us, waking up from the dream is a gradual, gentle process. Each time we decide to go within, to be, we practise living from soul, and in so doing we come to make more humane, more soulful, choices within the dream. We do not know how far we have travelled yet, and that is something we can accept. Some of us work with the process of living from soul for a long time, and can sometimes feel that we have made only slow progress, but what do we really know? How can we know what the benchmark is? Perhaps progress lies in the fact that we make better choices: that our choices come to be based more on love than on fear. Some of us will give up more easily than others, and some will never start at all. Do not measure yourself against others; do not judge your progress! Doing so is another way of connecting to fear by competing either against others or against some imaginary standard we uphold for ourselves.

We can apply our understanding of soulful living to life as we live now. With our gentle discipline of reminding ourselves and of re-establishing our soul perspective, we move forward. With our willingness, we initiate a lifelong process; our gentle discipline will keep us going, and life will reward us with more peace, joy and understanding.

Right Time, Right Age?

In the process of life, we often ask ourselves about the right timing.

I am too young to understand! I am too old to change my ways! Life is too complicated! I am busy! I am enjoying myself too much! It is not the right time! We can have many excuses for not living a soulful life. If we listen to them, we will never start to pay attention to our soul. We can start, however, at any time, even in this moment; maybe this book will serve as a reminder as you read it. Life presents many opportunities to us to remember, and all of us have the capacity to live from soul, each in our own unique way.

Adults are often taught by life that it is time to change, and this learning can sometimes come only with the maturing effect of experiencing many trials in life. These people come to a point where chasing life's many pleasures, such as power, prestige and entertainment, loses its allure. Often they feel an emptiness inside that makes them seek an additional dimension. They look, consciously or unconsciously, for a perspective of soul that allows them to enhance the life that they live, that tempers their desires and enriches their life at the same time. They have come to learn one of the fundamental lessons of soulful living: that less is more.

As we have said, many children do not have to work at living from soul. Young people, too, despite the distractions of their busy lives, can add a dimension of spiritual discipline to their life, even if only for 30 minutes a day, several times a week. As adults, we can always find the time to step back and readjust, if we choose to do so. It is very much a part of our habitual human lives that we often ignore that choice, but it is such a simple and easy choice to make! It begins simply with our willingness to work from a soulful perspective, and it is through our gentle discipline that we can continue to make the choice. This discipline helps us to re-establish living from our deeper nature, it alleviates stress and it helps us to deepen our sense of internal peace. In the western world we are all too easily distracted from the choice by the hectic nature of our daily lives. In contrast, in other, often poorer, countries, people start their days with a morning prayer or ritual or meditation. Through this, they express their gratitude to and for life. Every day of their lives begins with a centring in their deepest being. How many of us in western societies do this?

The choice to do so, however, is always present. We may slip from time to time, and forget, and that is okay. We can resume our focus at any time. We might need many attempts before we begin to notice how much joy and peace we experience when we centre ourselves in our soul. Such experience of greater peace and joy might lead us to develop an even deeper discipline: a more enduring but still gentle discipline that moves us further. Like so many of us, I have slipped often in my life; I have forgotten. It took me many years to seek, understand and develop my soul nature, and my journey, my story, is ongoing. While I do not know how far I have progressed (and that is an ignorance that does not matter at all), working with a soulful discipline has taught me many lessons: about modern life, about compassion for myself and others, and about patience and trust.

What Am I Entitled To?

Do you think that you are entitled to anything in life? Is it a quintessential part of our human experience to feel so entitled? After all, if we study hard, we should be entitled to an excellent job. If we work hard, we should be entitled to have money. If we live a correct and faithful life, we should be entitled to moral superiority. If we pray and act in a pious manner in our lives, we should be entitled to feel good about ourselves, and miracles should happen.

To live from a soulful perspective is to understand that life is really not about such entitlements. While we might live a life that is more consciously aware than others, this does not grant us moral superiority. We are neither superior nor inferior to those living less conscious lives, because we are all doing the best that we can with the faculties and level of understanding that we possess. Compassion is universal, no matter what our soul-alignment. Each of us brings compassion into our lives when we embody compassion ourselves: when we live it. All of us are indeed 'entitled' to freedom, joy, creativity and room for expression, but never at the expense of others.

We might all have known the feeling of entitlement, but so often that feeling is experienced through a filter of fear. When we feel and think we are entitled, we conjure up a universe that is not abundant. It can give to me, but not to others; it is not gracious enough to give to all. Subscribing to a non-abundant universe, we feel more entitled than others. We might work hard and believe that this gives us the right to condemn people who live on government benefits, even though we probably know nothing about why any individual person has had to make the choice to live on these small sums of money. We might participate socially and politically, and condemn others whom we perceive to be only 'vegetating'. These mistaken feelings of entitlement connect us with a feeling of need. We fear that the universe, our world, our society cannot meet the needs of all, but feel that our needs should be met as we have worked hard and have lived a morally upright life.

An aunt of mine was a nun in a Catholic order. Throughout her life she worked as a nurse, and in her later years she became a ward sister. She rose at four o'clock every morning for prayer in the church, worked from six o'clock for seven hours, rested for an hour or two, and then returned to the ward to work for a few more hours. She would spend much time sitting with cancer patients as they recovered or healed into death. My aunt devoted the whole of her life to care and service. In her late fifties, however, she was struck with Parkinson's disease and very quickly became dependent on her fellow sisters' care. My aunt complained to me that her illness made her feel utterly betrayed by life. After all, she had devoted herself to service, and so why did this illness come to her? Was she not entitled to live the later part of her life on Earth in peace and health as a just reward for her service? Her sense of entitlement caused her to rebel against the learning that life, her soul, was presenting to her through her illness. Sadly, as time and her illness progressed, my aunt became increasingly unaware of life and developed dementia. I do not know if she ever found peace with her illness and became able to let go of her sense of entitlement.

What is it that we are seeking when we feel entitled? Does life not provide us, in every moment, with exactly what we need in that moment? For most of us in the western world our basic needs for food, clothing, shelter and work are more than amply met. When we align the desires of our ego and personality with our soul, our needs are always met. We might only realise this in hindsight. We might not receive what we want, but we always receive what we need. Equally, our desires bring us always to where we are now.

If we yearn for peace in the external world, we need to connect with our peace within. We can extend our peace to others. When we do so, our internal peace becomes stronger and we serve as an example. If we want abundance, we simply connect with our own abundance, with ourselves as abundance. Abundance extends far beyond the material level. Abundance is present in our creative thoughts and feelings, and in the outpouring of love, compassion and joy that we feel. When we share the abundance that we have, it returns to us in multiple ways. Abundance from within is without limits. Perhaps the financial resources that we can share are limited, but the abundance of our heart and soul is unlimited. We can give our time to others in abundance: in, for example, the bliss that we experience in experiencing soul, in our compassion, in our acceptance of difference and our letting go of judging others, even when that is not easy. The ways are many.

We are not entitled to anything, but everything is a blessing. When we think that we are entitled to receive because we are doing the right deeds, we are expressing a belief in a specific order to our universe. This, however, is an order entirely of our own making. We want to control life, God, the universe, but can we actually ever control life?

Awareness of Life

Awareness of life means paying attention to the process of life. This includes paying attention on a daily basis to what is happening to us and how we choose to react to it. Awareness means observing how we react to the people with whom we engage and how we see ourselves in relation to them. It also means observing how we react to events on a wider scale: for example, how we react to potentially fear-inducing news from elsewhere in the world, brought to our attention by the media. Such news includes reports of earthquakes, wars or overwhelming national economic troubles.

When we become aware of life, we begin to develop our understanding of the workings of the world around us and of the people in it. By studying our own lives and our reactions to them, we also begin to understand who we are in each of the areas of life in which we participate. Each of us will play many roles: as a child, sibling, parent or partner, as a student or teacher, as a work colleague, as a member of society, as a citizen of our country, as an expression of our cultural heritage. We will also define ourselves in differing terms internally as our psychological and spiritual understanding of ourselves evolves and deepens over time.

Gradually, however, through the practising of awareness as life presents itself to us in each moment, we will reach a point of understanding, of knowing who we are at the deepest level: the level of soul, the level that lies beneath all the concepts of who we think we are. For those whose focus is largely on the material level, financial success and security might well be regarded as the most vital achievement in life. Equally, for those who focus on the 'spiritual' level, 'enlightenment' may be considered to be the most vital achievement. Is either, however, any more substantial than mist in the air? Both can come and disappear easily. Even if we think material success makes us 'happy', or at least 'comfortable', this might not be true if we dig deeper, and our possessions can easily disappear in the face of economic recession, job loss or illness. When we search for enlightenment, we are assuming that we have lost something that we must try very hard to find again, but isn't enlightenment just another concept?

If we choose to regard, feel and experience life from a concept of the total individuality of our ego/self, we can ignore a common and deeper connection to each other, to the world around us and to everything in that world. We can see life as a random series of events without any deeper meaning, but life offers us the choice to look behind these events. In the process of life, we have the opportunity to refocus on, embody and express our soulful qualities: unconditional love that helps us to embrace those we do not like at all; compassion that goes beyond 'feeling sorry' for someone and lets us feel the common ground we all come from; peace that leads to an inner calm, a relaxed and fluid body; joy that has no discernible origin but arises spontaneously, or a presence that expresses itself in an acute feeling and seeing of a situation. All this is possible when we decide to live life from soul. When we live like this, we are more able to let go of our expectations both of any given moment and of life overall.

In seeking to approach life with awareness, we face many challenges. These come to help us to develop other qualities: a courage that calls forth the strength to overcome our innate fears, a tenacity that helps us stick to our course despite difficult circumstances, and a perseverance that helps us to overcome obstacle after obstacle. Sometimes, we can only hold steady against the current of life with trust and faith. Such faith is not faith in a religious sense, but is what stays when everything, our illusions of grandeur and prestige and of need and inability to cope alike, has been stripped away.

In a life lived from a soulful perspective, we do not need a guru or a master teacher. It is all too easy to worship a guru and to forget that we are all equal: we are all souls experiencing what it is to be human. If we devote ourselves to a guru, we fail to live fully and directly, as we create in our image of the guru a filter between ourselves and our experience. If we worship a guru, we follow an inspiring example and we connect with a concept or system, but we do not listen to our own knowing, and it is our own knowing and only our own knowing that is, and expresses, soul teaching. When we abdicate responsibility and simply follow what our religion, our guru or our expectation of correctness stipulates, we live life as we think we 'should' live it instead of listening to our own inner signals. When we listen to our own process, we enlighten ourselves from moment to moment, situation to situation: we live a soulful life, and our humanity is enhanced. We follow our own unique path for soul living.

Our Impact on Others

Recently, a man stopped me as I was walking through the centre of the local town. The man was about 15 years my junior. He told me that his name was Faisal and that he had once worked for me as a member of one of the sales teams that I had managed about 12 years previously. Faisal instantly remembered my name, whereas I could only remember his face. I was surprised, pleased and a little perplexed that he had remembered me so clearly, when I could barely remember any detail of the circumstances in which we had worked together. I was intrigued, and, luckily, Faisal agreed to have a cup of coffee with me.

I did recall that one of my key tasks in that job had been to increase the number of staff in my team, as business had been buoyant. As we talked, Faisal revealed to me that at the time he had applied for the post within my team, he had been going through a very challenging period in his life. He had been cautioned by the police after getting into a brawl with someone who had insulted his sister, and he had also lost his long-term girlfriend, who had decided to return to her home country of Pakistan. Above all, Faisal had needed a job, guidance, something regular, to help him regain stability in his life. As we drank our coffee, he told me that what he remembered most about me from that time was my 'kindness' in the interview process and as his team leader afterwards.

While I hope that I have been able to show kindness many times over in the course of my life, I was surprised and pleased to hear that I had been able to have such a positive impact on Faisal. He told me that he believed that my treatment of him as an equal, my guidance, and my ability to accept who he was and his circumstances at that time had served as an inspiration to him. The job, the team and regular work had helped him to recover his life. This recovery had taken place over the course of the two years that he had stayed in the job. He had left the job shortly after I had left, because he had decided to start training as a chartered surveyor. He had also been able to recover a very good relationship with his father and had decided to enter the family business.

I felt truly touched by Faisal's memories of me, and so glad that I had been able to help him so much without realising that I had been doing so. Above all, what he told me that morning over coffee showed me just how much we can all impact others, even if we are unaware that we are doing so. If each of us were given the chance to look back at our lives to see the impact we have had on the people around us, many of us would be positively surprised. When we embody kindness and compassion, we do not know how we are positively influencing others even when we do not consciously intend to do so, even when we are completely unaware of it; we influence their lives positively simply by being who we are. Knowing this can make us far more alert to the impact we can have on others. Such knowledge is important, because our influence can also be negative if we act without an awareness that reminds us to tread lightly and to consider the results of our behaviour, actions and attitudes.

Imagine that at the point at which we leave this world we can watch a film replaying all of our actions and interactions. We would see how, over and over again, our family members, our work colleagues, our friends, even the checkout operators in our local supermarket or the other drivers on the road took their cue from us and went on to treat other people how we treated them. If we treated them kindly or with impatience, for example, their mood would change either way and they would treat others accordingly. We would also see that whenever we did not operate with awareness, we would be similarly affected by others' treatment of us. The film would help us to understand deeply that every choice in every moment, be it for kindness, generosity and compassion or for impatience, anger and selfishness, has a much wider impact than we think. While we might not pay attention to these aspects normally, knowing how much we do influence others, and how much they influence us, can alert us to the value of being more aware more often. We can make the decision to intend always to treat others with respect, and to do so independently of how we feel or of how our life is treating us. We can never truly know the full extent of our impact on the people around us, and to some extent this is beneficial; if we did know, the responsibility of that knowledge would be enormous. Even if we cannot fully know, however, we can choose to treat others in a positive, helpful way, so that our impact on them is likely to be a positive one, regardless of whether they or we are aware of the full nature of that impact.

Are We There Yet?

We might feel that life is asking us to take action, to perform in a certain way, but that we are not there yet. While on the outside we profess confidence and the wish to move forward, on the inside we feel angst-ridden. We can sense that we are being pushed forward by our soul, but our ego and personality scream that we are not yet ready. Equally, we might want to push forward from an ego impulse, but our deeper soul awareness also knows that we are not yet ready. That awareness knows that we first have to align our mind with our soul perspective: that we first have to allow our ego perspective to catch up with our deeper soul understanding.

Sometimes, when we feel we are not ready, it is because we lack trust in ourselves and in life. We are afraid that life will send us something that is too difficult or dangerous, or that demands that we change too much; we are afraid that life will send us something with which we will not be able to cope. If we can stop for a moment at these points of fear, however, and allow ourselves to drop down into our soul awareness, we will realise, always, that life will never send us a situation with which we cannot cope. Difficulties, on the contrary, are opportunities to acknowledge our innate capacity and potential, and to deepen our trust and understanding that life always presents challenges to us at the perfect moment: when we are ready for them. Acknowledging this, we can accept our fear but work with it, relax, breathe it away, transmute its energy into courage, trust and strength.

We might want to imagine that there is a 'future us' out there, one who has achieved what seems to be utterly unobtainable to us in the present moment because we are so overwhelmed by the fear of our own inadequacy. How would it feel if we were to step into the body of that confident, peaceful and wise 'future us' now? What would we look like? How would we behave? How would we hold ourselves, and what kind of body language would we use: would it express a different message from our body now? What kinds of clothes would we wear, and what colours? How would we talk and communicate? Would our facial expression look confident? Etc., etc. When imagining our 'future us' we can form a crisp, clear and strong picture in our mind. We can make it vibrant, dressed in colours and styles of clothing that we love and that we know suit us. We can picture ourselves standing erect, confident, but relaxed and loving at the same time. We look patient and happy to have arrived at who we are now.

Let us allow ourselves to stay with this picture for a while, to feel it deeply, to inhabit it fully, and then, when we are ready, to take it and place it in our hearts. Once it is firmly there, we can imagine the strength, the energy of the picture slowly flowing into the whole of the weak and inadequate person that we are afraid that we are now. As the picture flows into our mind and body – into our thoughts, emotions and ego – it begins to dissolve our fears into the illusions that they are, and the picture of clarity, vigour, wisdom and courage becomes exactly, and solely, who we are. Our soul is the creator and engine of this transformation, and it is our soul energy that creates the picture. As we stay with this process, we can feel the change becoming permanent: we can see and feel ourselves as already being that 'future' enhanced being. We can repeat this process many times, regularly, each time peeling back and dissolving a layer of fear. Each time we can ask ourselves what might need to happen for us to become our 'future self' already, and we can work with the answers that our soul will give to us. Perhaps we might need to undertake some form of training, or we might need to work on presenting ourselves. There might be some specific issues on which we will need to work; for example, healing and forgiveness, and a deep surrender, might be necessary. While there is no knowing how long it might take each of us to become our 'future us', we can already work with him/her on a regular basis; each of us brings forward the energy and necessary changes to the person that we each are now.

Soulful Living and Life as the Impetus for Change

Maurice and Roger

Maurice was a man who did not like to show his feelings. He held a lot of anger, not least about his childhood and parents, and about his enforced early retirement. He had four children and seven grandchildren with whom he greatly enjoyed spending time. One of his sons, Roger, had had a troubled past. He had experienced suicidal feelings for most of his life, was unwilling to work and did not want to participate in life very much at all.

The relationship between Maurice and Roger had been difficult since Roger had been a small boy, with Maurice finding Roger's behaviour during adolescence especially challenging. During that time, there had been shouting matches, extreme anger on both sides, Roger's use of enormous negative energy to demand Maurice's attention, and Maurice's response of almost complete rejection. Maurice was now in his late sixties and Roger in his early forties, and, sadly, very little of their interpersonal dynamic had improved. Maurice remained unable to show his love for Roger, or to give him the father's attention that Maurice knew he needed. All those years, Maurice seemed to have been overwhelmed by his own troubled past, and this had prevented him from being able to devote his energy to his son. Their relationship had settled into a state of mutual acceptance and tolerance, if that.

The anger trapped inside Maurice prevented him from accessing and experiencing, let alone living from, his loving, compassionate and trusting soul qualities. He chose, instead, to present a self-righteous and deeply cynical face to the world, spending most of his time watching television and pronouncing on his favourite subject: the dire state of the world.

Maurice was shaken out of his self-absorption, however, when Roger developed a severe illness that required him to spend a long period in hospital. Maurice and his wife began to spend a lot of time at their son's bedside, and this slowly had the effect on Maurice of causing him to look deeper within himself: to move beyond his concern with the external world to a place of contemplation and silence. Observing Roger's illness, and the suffering of the other patients in the hospital ward, Maurice began to feel compassion stirring within himself. He listened to the stories of the other patients, found himself empathising with them and felt a growing desire to help them wherever he could: a kind word here, a helping hand there. He found himself contemplating deeply the mystery of life that some people enjoy radiant health, while others seem to suffer terribly for no apparent reason.

Over time, Maurice found himself increasingly able to feel, and to express freely, his love for his son. His attitude towards life also changed: he began to exchange cynicism for compassion and hope. Roger too was changed positively by his experience of illness. The illness, in fact, had brought a further dimension to both of their lives: it allowed them to soften towards each other, to be at peace and to live more deeply from soul.

For all of us, there will have been times when we have felt ourselves to be completely stuck: when it has seemed as if there is nothing in our lives that can help us to move forward. So often, however, it is just at the point at which we are resigning ourselves to living a half-lived, difficult life that life will provide us with the necessary impetus in the form of an unexpected circumstance. An event will happen, a crisis such as Roger's illness, perhaps, that stirs us into action. It propels us into a deeper exploration of our inner selves, propels us towards our soul perspective of compassion, love, joy, acceptance and peace, and away from our closed-off fear, cynicism and pain. It is never too late for this change to occur. Life can look hopeless, but all of a sudden the transformation comes about. The crisis, in fact, is a gift.

In the World but Not Of It

Many of us seek to conform, if only partially, to what is considered to be acceptable in our society. As human beings we are social animals and so our natural wish is to be at peace, rather than at odds, with the world. It is perfectly possible for each of us, however, to live in this world from a perspective of soul. Yes, each of us is the sum total of what we have become in our human life, but we are also so much more than the product of the interactions between our ego-mind and body. As we have said, our ego-mind and body, our lives as we choose to live them, the game of life as we choose to play it are not who we are. They are, rather, simply the tools through which we operate and through which, by that operation, we come to know the essence of ourselves, who we really are: our soul.

Through the simple discipline of acknowledging our nature as soul on a regular basis, we can take enormous strides forward. Each moment of acknowledgement helps us to drop down deeper into our true self, to become a fuller, more individuated person. When we choose to live from soul, we choose to live from our divine centre, i.e. the expression of the creative life force, source, chi, prana, God, love, the Is (we may give it whatever name best suits us) that is the essence of who we are, that animates us and that we experience through our consciousness and through the exhilarating aliveness of our being. When we choose a soul perspective, we also connect with and recognise others who are seeking their truth, who are choosing to live from their true centre. As we all live from soul, we also find ourselves bringing soulful experiences into our lives and into the lives of those around us, in the form, for example, of synchronicities, meaningful happenstances and opportunities for compassion, service and joy.

For all of this, we simply need an open heart. We might study and amass a mountain of intellectual knowledge, but our heart can still be empty. A person who has an articulate, well-trained and vigorous mind can communicate learned knowledge devastatingly well, but their heart can be a cold, dark place, starved of light and closed off by a scepticism that has petrified into cynicism. As we have discussed, life will always offer us the opportunity to go within to discover and revitalise our heart: perhaps disaster strikes, or our belief in our indomitable ability to achieve whatever we want is shattered, or someone whom we cannot live without chooses to leave us, or we are overcome with debilitating sickness. There are so many ways in which sorrow can arrive in our lives, and when it comes deeply enough we might seek to understand the reasons for it, but this intellectual understanding will not be enough to help us to survive the pain. When we live from soul, however, we will receive the necessary answers, the necessary growth in wisdom. When we drop down into our open heart, we will find there the instinctive, innate, universal wisdom of soul. We simply need to practise listening to that wisdom. We need to allow our heart centre to develop by centring ourselves within it, because it is in our open heart that we truly come to feel and know our soul.

With an open heart, soul can truly shine through our human experience. We feel protected and inspired by it. It changes us, and as we allow ourselves to be changed, we change everything around us. We feel truly connected to our world, and we come to see life as a co-creative process: we create with all others. Life is a delightful paradox:

we need a human life to truly experience ourselves as soul, and in living our life we imbue it with soulful qualities. Only through living our life from soul do we become fully human. In our interaction with others we manifest our soulful qualities and come to realise our human potential; we can only realise this potential by engaging with each other. Through these interactions, we also come to recognise ourselves in others and to understand that we are all mirrors for each other, and that indeed, ultimately, there is no other; we are all one.

Throughout the existence of *homo sapiens sapiens* much thought has been given to the spiritual 'purpose' of our existence. All that we can know is that we are conscious beings engaged in the experience of life and learning a little, or a lot, of wisdom from it. We also know that there are many levels to our consciousness: many levels within ourselves from which we can choose to interact with life. This book's purpose is to describe what it is like to live from the deepest level of soul. Why does creation exist? What is the nature of the creative force, prana, chi, God, source? These are questions to which we can only propose answers. We cannot anthropomorphise the nature of creation. It is in our nature to seek to posit the existence of the 'Mind of God': to believe, for example, that we are 'God's fingers', and that through us 'God' is experiencing itself. It is probably true to say, however, that, if the 'Mind of God' exists, its workings are very likely to be beyond the comprehension of our human minds.

When we drop down into soul, however, and live and experience from the deepest part of ourselves, we can sense, beyond our capacity to squash it into language, a deep spiritual or divine meaning to our existence and experience. There, we live in a place of love, innate understanding, compassion, acceptance, clarity and peace, which in its beauty and vastness feels to our intuition as if it could be an expression of 'the Mind of God'. Soul consciousness is a sublime sense which, when we live from it, enables us to interact with the world and our human selves in loving, healing ways. That is, surely, all we need to understand about our spiritual purpose.

Each of us is responsible for our actions in life, and for our life itself; it is up to each of us to create a life lived well, and to work together to create a loving, peaceful, harmonious human existence in the world. When we live from soul, we can let go of the destructive fear that can breed greed, violence and anger when we live only from the ego-mind. Everything that manifests, everything that exists, including ourselves and the universe in which we live, is an expression of the creative force. Each manifestation affects the wellbeing of all the others. We each have a profound effect on each other and on the planet on which we live. The more that we come to live more and more deeply from soul and the greater the numbers in which we do so, the more we will all ensure the wellbeing of the whole.

Life is a dance during which, through our human existence, we learn to live from soul and to understand who we truly are. Yes, we each have a story, the story of an individualised life, but this story is not who we are; it is merely the dance that we have chosen, through which, as we perfect the steps through experience and practice, we come to find our true selves. The inevitable movement of the dance through fear, for example, helps us to understand love and to prefer to express love, to receive love, indeed to be love. Paradise on Earth is simply living in peace with each other and the Earth as one reality, expressing our soulful qualities in all our encounters with life, understanding that I am you and you are me. With each difficult circumstance in life, we have the opportunity to choose a soulful perspective, and through this choice, through performing the dance, we allow love to come into the world.

Ultimately, we already are what we seek. Our desires are only an expression of wanting to find our way home, and home is oneness, and oneness is here now in all that is. We only need to adjust our perspective, to live from soul, in order to see it. We do not need to go anywhere else. We do not have to become anything else. We always have the potential to express unconditional love, and it is our choice whether to perpetuate this in our life or not. We are always able to choose to live from soul rather than from the conditioned reflexes that we have learnt from living an unconscious life. The choice in every moment is ours, and only ours, to make.

Often in life, we will have had the feeling that something is not working. A particular condition or circumstance has caused us to feel stuck, and to become, perhaps, consumed with self-doubt. Each of these sensations of 'stuckness' is simply a signal to drop down into our soul, to operate from an open heart and, above all, to choose love. The more we choose a soulful perspective, the fewer the stuck-moments will become. We might see an agonising gap between the actual and the ideal in our journey from here to there, but that is okay.

Our job is to help each other; the more we have worked on ourselves, the better a mirror we are to those around us, because they can see themselves in us and in our actions, and they can learn from us, as we, indeed, can learn from them. We can practise courtesy and kindness, and help others to unlock their specific door to love and humanity. Through this process, we lose our confused ego-mind 'human' selves and find our true, loving 'soul' selves more strongly. By living through our human qualities we become 'divine'. By acknowledging our divine origin, we become truly human.

Acceptance of Life

As a baby, we come into life with nothing. We are aware of our natural body needs, and, normally, those needs are met, and we are cared for and loved. We are defenceless. We can make a great deal of noise if we are unhappy or in pain, but we are only beginning to learn our brains and bodies, and so have little choice but to accept what is happening to us. Luckily, as babies and toddlers, we have a natural trust and acceptance of life. We are naturally open, happy and loving, and we accept life as it comes. Our mental concepts and habitual emotional responses to life will develop later, but at this age our hearts are open and we operate naturally with the awareness of soul. As children, we are still strongly connected to the essence of who we are; we still largely live from and express our soul. While we cannot yet articulate this, we live it. We trust our parents to look after us. We see life as a wonderful adventure, and we have the patience to explore and grow.

As we grow, our intellectual understanding of and emotional responses to the world also grow. We learn to compare ourselves with others, and begin to experience difference and separation. We see what others have and what we do not have, and we begin to undergo the human experience of envy, fear, desire and competition. This is a natural process. Our desires develop as we learn about prestige, fame, power and money, and that is fine. Desires are the tools of our ego-mind, and they make us want to stride out into the world: to explore, experience, survive, strive and succeed, and to find our place in the world. All the while, we are comparing ourselves to others, and, depending on the degree of our self-judged success or failure in this respect, our willingness to be content with, to accept what is in our life often begins to diminish.

For some of us, this will engender a deep feeling of loss. When we look at small children and the way in which they can be lost in a game of make-believe or be enraptured by the beauty of a flower, we realise that we have exchanged the joyful, pure, loving, optimistic acceptance of life that we used to have as children for the tension and anxiety of adulthood. Yes, as adults we have achieved much; we have taken full advantage, for example, of the freedom to pursue the life that we want, and we have been successful in our careers, honed our intellects, fallen in love, raised healthy families, but for some of us a feeling of loss will always be present underneath life, below the surface of our daily awareness. This sense of loss is a message from our soul: a simple reminder that, whilst we can stay committed to the way of life we live, as we have a living to earn and a mortgage to pay etc., we can change our perspective at the same time – away from the externally-focussed, fear-based thinking of our ego-mind to the loving perspective of soul. The sense of loss is a reminder to live from soul, rather than solely from the tools of the ego-mind and body.

As discussed, the game of life will offer us other reminders: a force of nature that makes us lose our possessions; a stock market crash that propels us into bankruptcy; an accident, a debilitating illness or the onset of old age that makes us lose our agility, health and beauty. When we see well-known actors many years after the films that made them famous, we are often shocked at how much they have aged: at how little they resemble the beautiful younger selves that were captured on film. We see through the illusion then, and understand that they are simply human: that they are as vulnerable to encroaching old age and death as we are. When you look in the mirror these days, do you ever have the feeling that the face that you are seeing cannot be yours? I certainly do. Inside, I am ageless and feel that hardly any time has passed since my twenties, but when I look in the mirror I see a wrinkled and middle-aged man: one with more lines and less hair, but, I hope, a face that displays a more relaxed and peaceful attitude towards life.

That face in the mirror is simply another call to live from soul. There is a beauty in the lines of aging, and the wisdom they express, which we can see easily if we let go of our conditioned responses to life and look with the loving perspective of soul. Life is a beautiful and impermanent process. Those lines remind of us of that. They remind us to be glad of this wonderful life, and to live it fully with joy and love in every moment of its passing.

Judy

Judy, a teacher, always looked sad, so much so that deep lines of sorrow had become engraved upon her face. Colleagues often wondered about the terrible burden that she must be carrying, but they said nothing to her. They dared not ask. After all, prod a hornets' nest and you might have difficulty dealing with the result. One day, however, the school held a seminar for its teachers on 'solution-centred' therapy. Within the safety of the seminar, Judy finally confided that she had lost her only son. She was trying to live not only with the pain of that unbearable loss, but also with the equally unbearable rage that she felt at the fact that he had died not through an accident, or some freak instance of fate, but through human carelessness. He had been killed by an act of common negligence during a routine hospital operation.

What is the answer to such pain?

Distance can allow some of us to temper our compassion. Somehow, we can store away natural disasters that we learn about in the news. We respect and admire those who flock to help, but we feel disconnected from it all. The physical distance of a natural disaster enables an emotional distance in ourselves. Too much negative news can even desensitise us to such tragedies. After all, we need to focus all our energies on our own daily challenges and difficulties. For others of us, however, the footage of tremendous loss, fear and suffering helps us to re-connect instantly with our compassion, and we become fully engaged, donating whatever we can to help.

When our hearts are touched by the pain and misery being experienced by other living beings, our empathy with their situation helps us to rise above ourselves, and we truly live from soul in those moments of oneness and compassion. When disasters are physically far away, however, it is all too easy for us to return to our comfortable normal lives after a short period of time.

It is a different experience, though, when we are confronted with the pain of the personal disaster of a friend, relative or colleague. We see their pain every day, and we cannot distance ourselves from it. What piece of advice could we have given to Judy, to ourselves, or to anyone finding themselves in such a heartbreaking and difficult situation? How do we even know how it is appropriate to act when confronted with such an event?

When we resist life, we create stress. Accepting our experiences in life does not mean that we cannot change our lives. It allows us, rather, to see what needs to be changed, and to be kind to ourselves by understanding that changing our lives, and our perception of our lives, is a journey. In Judy's case, she could not undo the tragic loss of her son, nor could she make sense of why he had to die in such a way. All she could do was choose her attitude to her loss. All she could do was choose not to allow it to cause her to live each day as if it were her own living death. All she could do was choose to make peace with it, to love her precious son through her cherished memories of him, to live her life with joy and enthusiasm because he could not, and to show compassion for those whose mistakes had caused his death, who were likely to be in their own kind of living death because of their guilt at those mistakes and who, because of her son's death, would come to do everything in their power to ensure that such mistakes would become impossible for anyone to make again.

As the psychiatrist Viktor Frankl explained in his world-famous work *Man's Search for Meaning*, about his experiences in a World War II concentration camp: when everything that we know and hold dear has been stripped away, what alone remains is 'the last of human freedoms', i.e. the ability to 'choose one's attitude in a given set of circumstances'.[24] In the existential theory of 'logotheraphy' that Frankl lived by and began to develop through his experiences in the camp, it is the striving to find a meaning in one's life that is the primary, most powerful motivating force in our lives. Frankl believed that our lives have meaning even under the most desperate of circumstances, and that, further, we have absolute freedom to find meaning in what we do and what we experience, or at least in the stand we take when faced with a situation of unchangeable suffering. Those who survived the camp, and those of us who are able to survive in our own lives no matter how impossible the circumstances seem, are able to do so because we choose our attitude: we create some form of meaning from events. Nothing has an intrinsic meaning. It only has the meaning that we give to it. Acceptance of life from the soul, through an open heart, therefore, is more than a passive resignation. It is, rather, an attitude towards life, an active engagement with it, a deep knowing.

---

[24] London: Random House/Rider, 2004

Acceptance is not about the passive condoning of human actions that cause hurt, pain and death. Far from it! It is an acknowledgement that such actions happen, that humans still have a capacity to engage in war, rape and slavery, and in the infliction of suffering on others and on themselves. Acceptance enables us to avoid being annihilated by suffering. Acceptance, compassion and the courage to endure, and to help to create change, come from soul. When we choose a soulful perspective in each moment, we begin to shift the world.

If we wish to stop war in the world, let us begin by working to eliminate the war within ourselves, to practise working from soul, from the still place of quiet peace within us. If we were all to work on this, human-induced suffering in the world would begin to lessen, and would eventually cease. All suffering and belligerence starts within us, and as individuals we create war together. We need peace inside a sufficient number of us to create a tipping point from which peace spreads across the whole world.

Acceptance also means that we allow ourselves to fully feel difficult, uncomfortable feelings such as grief, sadness, anger or bitterness. The 'I' of the soul in each of us can stand back and observe the emotional, thinking 'me' experiencing such feelings. The 'I' knows that it is not the feelings, but also knows that the 'me' needs to acknowledge them completely in order to be able to let them go. In our hectic daily lives, we tend to develop the habit of 'bottling up' or 'pasting over' difficult feelings because we do not have time for them. We have time only to find quick remedies to 'touchy' situations. Acceptance embraces all areas of our life. When we accept feelings such as grief and sadness, when we observe them from the point of view of soul, we allow a potential transformation of these feelings into peace, joy and wisdom, because we know that these feelings and the events that caused them are simply transitory moments in our lives. Peace, however, stays with us, no matter what the future brings; it is a peace with the process of life. Joy comes with the awareness that we are changing: that we are finding the wisdom to accept the unacceptable.

To return to Judy: there was no answer to and no relief from her grief in the way that she craved. Neither she nor her son could ever receive 'justice' for his death due to human failure. Grieving is a natural process; suffering, however, is a choice. Suffering can be an overwhelming experience, but it is a doorway to profound soul understanding. Through suffering, we begin to see the wider vista of life; we learn to grieve, but not to suffer.

James

For too many years, James had felt terribly lonely. He yearned for a companion who would love and care for him, who would truly 'see' him, and who would accept him for exactly who he was without question. With a mixture of fear, hope and desperation, he had recently joined a dating website, and had had contact with several women, but he had yet to find anyone with whom he sensed a connection. In the evenings now, he had taken to sitting at home contemplating the misery of his life. He felt the loneliness as a physical ache in his chest. The emotion was so strong that it was almost overpowering. In an effort to escape it, James watched television and DVDs, and drank too much whisky and red wine, but when the bottles were empty, and the programmes and films were finished, the feeling remained. He went to bed early to switch it off. James had no mechanisms to deal with the strength and pain of his feelings.

As the dating website appeared to have failed him, he decided next to seek the help of a life coach. In his sessions with the coach, James discovered that he made no effort to sustain his relationships with the few friends that he had managed to keep. He also came to realise that he was extremely unhappy and bored in his current job. Overall, he began to see that, rather than approaching life assertively, his habit was to approach it with a dull passivity.

Inspired by his life coach, James decided to join a dancing group to have fun and to meet new people. He also enrolled in a course at the local college to improve his qualifications so that he could find a better job. James had come to understand that he had projected the blame for his boredom and lack of inspiration onto something else: his lack of a companion in life. By doing so, he had completely failed to take responsibility for his own life. James had come to understand, at the soul level, that only by embracing that responsibility and acting accordingly could he achieve the happiness that he wanted.

His participation in the dancing club quickly made him feel much better. It was an excellent beginning. James had still to find a loving companion, but he found himself feeling happy to be out in the world. He also now knew what to do if the loneliness began to ache in his chest. He did not try to numb it with the television or alcohol, but contacted one of his friends instead. James had begun to work on accepting his situation in life. He had finally taken responsibility for creating his life, and was now beginning to transform it into the life that he wanted it to be. His acceptance of the state of his life, and of his responsibility for it, now empowered him, allowing him to begin to change his life for the better.

When we resist life, we are expressing a lack of trust in its process. We might tell ourselves that some of our experiences are worthwhile but others are not. As we will all have found, however, so often it is the very experiences that we do not like, the ones that are difficult, embarrassing, uncomfortable or hard, that bring us the most learning and wisdom, that teach us the most. When we live from soul, we know that all experiences are welcome, and we invite all experiences into our lives because we know that they will cause us to grow and develop our soul qualities of love, compassion, joy, clarity and peace. If we live from soul, we embrace everything that occurs in our lives, knowing that life will never bring us something with which we cannot cope.

Acceptance is a powerful expression of living from soul, and it is a powerful tool. It enables us to move increasingly away from the restriction of fear-based emotions, and at the same time it increases our awareness of our creative power. The more we come to approach life with acceptance, the less we will respond to life's events with debilitating stress. Acceptance enables us to learn through all of our experiences and to regard them all as equally precious, because through each of them we become more finely tuned to living from soul. Each experience allows our compassion and love for ourselves, and for others, to grow. We become a friend to all that we are, and to all that is in the world.

Trust and Patience

In the process of accepting life, we develop trust and patience. Trust comes through our understanding that whatever comes into our life in any moment is exactly the learning that we need in that moment. Patience comes because we understand that we have the capacity, the creative power and clarity to work through any situation, and the knowledge and faith that it will be resolved at exactly the right time.

Sometimes, life can seem like an unending series of almost impossible challenges.

Kim

Kim endured a heartbreaking divorce. She had fallen head over heels for her now ex-husband Ben and had committed herself totally to their relationship. Theirs had been a whirlwind romance, and they had married within five months of their first meeting. In that short time, Kim had noticed Ben's fondness for alcohol and quickness of temper, but she had been sure that she and the stability of marriage would tame him.

Within barely two years of their marriage, Ben and Kim had two children. Their life was very comfortable. Kim looked after the children and the house, whilst Ben led a busy, successful life as a stock market trader. There was no shortage of money, and they had a wealthy lifestyle, with a beautiful, large house and many holidays abroad.

Ben, however, continued to drink large quantities of alcohol and was often aggressive to Kim, especially if he felt under pressure at work because one of his deals had failed to work out. Occasionally, he would actually hit her, but he would barely remember doing so, because he had invariably been drunk. At first, Kim believed that she would be able to help Ben to stop abusing alcohol and hurting her. She tried to persuade him to enter therapy so that he could address his anger and alcohol abuse, and also suggested that he look for a different, less stressful job. Kim even offered to go back to work herself, in order to relieve Ben of some of the responsibility of supporting the family financially. Ben rejected all of these suggestions, however, and his abuse of Kim steadily worsened.

After eight years of marriage, Kim knew that she could no longer bear this treatment, and she filed for divorce. Ben refused to cooperate, became even more abusive and threatened to cut Kim off from all their money. Their divorce proceedings dragged on, as Ben took delight in being as obstructive as possible. He missed appointments and refused to give Kim any financial support for the children, so she had to rely on handouts from her family and friends. Kim felt completely overwhelmed by all the difficulties in her life; not only was Ben's behaviour insupportable, but their children were also suffering because of it. Their young son began wetting his bed, and their daughter became increasingly wilful, stubborn and difficult.

It took two dreary, hard and difficult years for the divorce to be finalised, and even then Ben still did everything possible to avoid his financial obligations to the children. At this time, Kim found herself plummeting into what she came to call a 'dark night of the soul'. She spent as much time as possible reading and contemplating, seeking to understand why this painful and difficult trial had come into her life. She worked hard on developing a trust within herself that her life would mend, and that learning, transformation, and a far better, wiser and more peaceful life would come from it all. After many months of this soul-level examination of her life, Kim decided that she wanted to train as a counsellor for divorcing couples, so that she could use her experience to help others to find a less painful way through separation. After several years' training, Kim became a fully qualified, effective and compassionate counsellor who, through this process, had become totally healed from, and at peace with, her past.

As babies, we have an innate trust in the world; we know at the soul level that life, the creative force, seeks only to love and nurture us. As we grow, however, our emotional capacity to trust becomes tempered by our experiences. It is strengthened when we are treated with love, compassion and respect, and it can be shattered if those whom we trust let us down. Our experience and understanding of soul-level trust is developed and shaped through the challenges that we face. The learning of patience is an integral part of that process. Trust means that we have the patience to work through the challenges of life, because we know that those challenges are opportunities to deepen our understanding and wisdom, and to move more and more into operating only from the clarity and peace of soul. Patience is a knowing that all will be right and well for us, even if, in this moment, we cannot yet see the solution to our problems. Trust is the kernel of soul wisdom within a disaster that says we will pass through it no matter what. Our awareness of patience grows as our awareness of trust grows. We embrace, embody and express patience when we live from the trust that is at the core of who we are. Trust without patience falters. Patience without trust will abandon the game early and refuse to try again.

How do life's difficulties appear when we view them with the trust, patience and peace of our soul understanding? Accepting these difficulties is more than just smiling at the challenges they present. It is, rather, about embracing those challenges, knowing that deep within ourselves we have ample resources of wisdom and guidance that will enable us to move forward to achieve resolution. We know that challenges are to be welcomed, because they help us to deepen our peace. We know that, however difficult the challenge we face, we can still find joy in the moment, in a stranger's smile, in the warmth of sunshine on our skin, in the laughter of children, in the feeling of wellbeing and gratitude for life that, when we truly live from soul, resides effortlessly within our hearts.

Feeling Helpless

Accepting life's challenges also means accepting our feelings of helplessness. Sometimes, life can present us with a challenge that seems insurmountable, with which we feel completely ill-equipped to deal, from which we can see no way out. Circumstances such as these demand our true trust and patience, because they require us simply to acknowledge the situation and to wait. They require us to accept that we do not have to have all of the answers now, but that the answers will come when they, and we, are ready.

Answers come through the process of life. Perhaps first our understanding needs to deepen, or our willingness or courage to grow. Many of us can recognise in hindsight those periods in our lives when our inner resources had to grow to catch up with the demands that life was making upon us. Those demands often come in the expectations that other people have of us. We can feel helpless under the weight of those expectations, and sometimes liberation and moving forward come when we learn to be true to and operate from our true soul selves and to say 'no'.

Barbara

Barbara's father was an alcoholic, and so she had been largely raised by a mother who despised him and who did everything in her power to convince Barbara that, as all men were as weak and untrustworthy as her father, Barbara had to become as strong and self-reliant as possible. Throughout her adult life, Barbara moved from one romantic relationship to another, frequently picking self-absorbed men with a tendency to self-pity and a fondness for alcohol. These men always regarded Barbara as a pillar of strength, and indeed she would always go out of her way to rescue them from the self-created difficulties in which they found themselves. One boyfriend was addicted to gambling, and so Barbara plundered her bank account to pay his debts. Another, a mature student, had been too lazy and disorganised to complete the research necessary for his final thesis, and so Barbara dropped everything to do the research and finish the thesis for him.

By her early forties, Barbara was a highly experienced schoolteacher and a single parent with two children. She had come to prefer to live without a partner, because, just as her mother had, she had come to loathe weak, emotionally incontinent and seemingly helpless men, and she had also come to suspect that either all men were like this or she could only attract those that were. Barbara was very aware of the influence of her mother's dictums and her father's example in this regard, and she also knew that her mother's dictums had become self-fulfilling prophecies in Barbara's own life: she had always chosen weak and helpless men as partners. Barbara still yearned deeply for a loving, worthy companion, but she had given up. Life was simpler, and less disappointing, living on her own with her children.

One day, Barbara was attending a meeting with colleagues when she discovered that one of them, Graham, was suffering from cancer and would soon have to go into hospital for an urgent operation. Graham closely fitted Barbara's male stereotype. Male and female colleagues alike regarded him as weak and embarrassingly over-emotional. He cried easily and often.

At the meeting, Barbara, like most of her colleagues, felt awkward and helpless around Graham. She had always been able to express soul-level qualities of love and compassion easily, and would have liked very much to console Graham, but her mother's training, reinforced by her own experience of men, set in, and she found herself unable to vocalise her sympathy and support for him. At the meeting, therefore, Graham felt himself to be completely isolated. Barbara and the others felt too awkward to encourage him and to wish him luck.

The fate of others can challenge us, especially if it creates within us a deep embarrassment at our failure to react appropriately. Sometimes, we simply do not have the answers, either for ourselves or for others. At other times, fear might make us unable to express sympathy, as someone else's fate might remind us too sharply of the uncertainty of our own lives. Sometimes, we are afraid to act because we might say the wrong thing, or because our compassion might be misinterpreted or rejected.

If we really do feel unable to express our compassion openly, however, we can always do so in our heart, silently wishing the person whom we want to help on their journey well. When we express compassion in our hearts because we cannot find the right words to say with our voice, we are also expressing compassion for ourselves for our inability to express our love and care in words. As we send out our compassion to others, so will others be sending their compassion to us, for we are one human race and we all face similar stories.

There will be times when we cannot find an active compassion for others, or for ourselves, in our hearts. What do we do then? It is at these times that our soul wisdom shows us that there is a subtle, gentle compassion in refusing to judge, to look down on or to pity ourselves or others in times of difficulty, whether these are self-inflicted or not. Sometimes, the best, most meaningful compassion that we can give is simply to let each other, or ourselves, be.

Soulful Living and Love

Unconditional Love

We are surrounded by unconditional love, whether we respond to it or not. At the soul level, we *are* unconditional love, and we can live, move, think, feel and express ourselves from that love whenever we choose to live from soul. We can imbue all that we are and do with the energy of unconditional love, from giving a hug to a stranger in distress to working with focus to produce a much-needed report, to tucking our children into bed with a loving kiss, to cleaning our home with loving attention.

When we live from soul, we also love and accept ourselves unconditionally. If we do not, we are likely to attract someone into our lives who will confirm to us that we feel worthy only of a conditional love. Such a person will mirror and reinforce any sense of self-unworthiness that we might have. In contrast, when we do love and accept ourselves unconditionally, we will attract a person who also loves themselves in this way and who is, therefore, ready, able and willing to love us unconditionally too. When we love ourselves and others unconditionally, we do not need other people to confirm who we are; we know who we are, and we free ourselves and those around us from any expectations that we could have of them, because any expectation that we have means that we have put a condition on our love. Equally, we do not need other people to love us to make us feel whole.

We are whole; we have everything we are. Unconditional love from soul is spontaneous, innate, wise and easy. It is also liberating and energising for everyone who expresses and receives it.

Any situation we draw to ourselves enables us to practise living and reacting from our soul core of unconditional love. From that core we can give and receive freely, joyously, knowing that we are safe and that we will receive from life far more than we can ever give. We can also enjoy silence, because we have no fearful need to fill the void with noise; instead, we can find the meaning, wisdom and clarity that reside in silence. When we live from unconditional love, we come to understand the hidden meaning in the situations that we encounter, whether they be wonderful or difficult. Living from unconditional love, we find that our wisdom, trust, patience and acceptance grow and, as they do so, our suffering diminishes, because we increasingly come to understand the simplicity of play in the material world.

A flower is connected to everything around it. It draws life from the sun's light, the gases in the air, and the minerals and water in the soil; without them, it cannot grow and blossom. As I write this, I can see that a two-metre-tall sunflower is drinking in the light in a garden. This radiantly beautiful plant with its thick stem and plethora of leaves grew from one tiny flat brown seed. All of its beauty and strength lay latent in that seed, and when the time comes for the flower to rot back into the earth, all of the strength and beauty that it once was will be contained in its own seeds, ready to burst into radiant life again come the return of summer. We are like the sunflower and its seeds.

We are so often taught to think of ourselves as individual beings, each completely separate from the other and from the world around us, but we are not separate. We carry the genetic codes passed on through our ancestors through thousands of years, and we will give these genes to our own offspring, as they will give them to theirs, and in each generation new genetic interconnections have been and will be made. Our ancestors live within us, as do our successors. We live on the Earth, and, as with the sunflower, the Earth and the sun give us life. The Earth is part of the universe, and the carbon and other elements of which our bodies are made come from that universe. The universe is ever expanding. The Earth is replete with fecund life. The primordial creative force is everywhere, informing the universe and everything within it, including us. We are 'stardust' expressions of that creative force. We are part of everything, and everything is a part of us. This being so, our only possible response to the manifestations of the creation that we are around us is one of unconditional love.

Love for Ourselves and Love for Others

Recently, I came across a press article about Mother Teresa, the Albanian Catholic nun who founded the Missionaries of Charity in Calcutta in

1950 and who for more than 45 years oversaw that organisation's care of the poor, sick, orphaned and dying in India and 122 other countries. Among its work, the Missionaries of Charity established hospices, schools, orphanages, homes for people suffering from various diseases, soup kitchens, and children's and family counselling programmes. Such was the esteem in which Mother Teresa was held by governments and the Catholic Church alike that she received prestigious awards both from the Indian Government and internationally, including the Nobel Peace Prize in 1979, and was beatified as Blessed Teresa of Calcutta by Pope John Paul II following her death in 1997.

'Mother Teresa' has become something of a byword for 'selflessness' in our society, and, indeed, I noticed the article and took the time to read it because it was seeking to question whether or not she had been quite as selfless as she had appeared. The article made interesting reading, but I was not convinced that it had achieved its aim of casting vigorous doubt on Mother Teresa's motivation. I came to the conclusion that the larger issue behind the article, and the reason that it had presented itself to me, was the profound reminder that Mother Teresa and others like her give to us simply by how they choose to behave in the world. An article like this, whatever its critical intent, reminds us not to put ourselves first, but, rather, to move ourselves out of the way so that we can live lives usefully expressing our love and compassion for those around us.

Such a laudable goal is very easy to state, but how can we fulfil it if we have not first learnt to treat ourselves with compassion, love and kindness? We can truly look after others selflessly only when we first look after ourselves. If we do not, we are not able to give genuine, selfless love and compassion, but only a pale facsimile of it. This is because our lack of love for ourselves will keep us focussed on ourselves, even if we are not aware of it. We will not be able to be totally with the other person. Our lack of love for ourselves will filter through our behaviour and responses to the person in need: as an impatience, as a shortness of temper, as a too-frequent talking about oneself.

Would we entrust our emotional, mental or physical wellbeing to a therapist who was, say, only 18 years old, and who therefore lacked experience and wisdom in the ways of the world and the human psyche? Yes, perhaps, if it were purely a light physical massage that we were seeking, but what if we needed a psychotherapist or a grief counsellor? Would we be comfortable entrusting our problems to someone who has not yet had the opportunity to live enough to understand our experiences and the sophisticated complexity of our relationship to our internal and external worlds?

The will to help and to give compassion and love are wonderful, innate soul qualities, but, without the wisdom of life experiences to inform them, their expression can feel hollow, trite, even patronising. The right words might be said, and we might even hear them, but they cannot carry the energy of genuine wisdom and compassion that would help us to trigger the necessary internal changes within ourselves. Genuine compassion and love for ourselves, and then for others, develop over time, through the experience of life's joys and sorrows. They have their own natural pace of becoming, and they cannot be pushed or faked.

When each of us, be we a friend, a parent, a therapist or Mother Teresa, expresses genuine love, compassion and care for another, all we are ever being is a potential aid for change. If we are able to express genuine love and compassion, it is because we have arrived at a point in our lives where we have found, accepted and embodied the compassion and love for ourselves that is our, and everyone's, true soul nature, and so we can now share our nature freely with others. All we can ever do is share.

In expressing our compassion and care for others in pain, we might help to trigger within them their own willingness and energy to work on the changes that are necessary in their lives. Only they can achieve those changes. Their lives will provide the context for change, and their trust, patience and self-loving wise action will move them forward by helping them to connect with their own soul qualities of self-love and compassion.

As human beings we tend to compare ourselves, our rate of progress, with each other. Doing so can make us feel inadequate or superior. This tendency to compare is a block to our experience and expression of soul-level compassion and love for ourselves and for others. We might not be able, yet, to achieve total self-compassion and selflessness, but we can accept that, whilst there are differences between all of us, we are all on a similar journey through life: we were all born, we are all growing old, and we will all die. We are all, therefore, able to share the love we have for ourselves, as little as that might be. Each of us grows into self-compassion and compassion for others at our own pace. Change might take a few weeks, months or many years, and we can be certain that any expectation as to when we should reach the end of that journey will only lead to disappointment. True soul-level love and compassion express themselves, above all, through being gentle with ourselves.

The more we choose to live from and express our soul qualities, the more our experience and the strength of our expression of those qualities will increase over time. We will be able to show simple acts of compassion, and to feel more love for ourselves. At every stage, we can embody and trust the love that we are, however that love looks to us, and we can encourage others to do so as well. We can be grateful, too, if our egos slip into making comparisons that leave us feeling that our progress in being and expressing love is inadequate, because that feeling will serve as a gentle reminder to search deeper within ourselves to find our love.

Pleasing Others

Some of us live our whole lives without ever knowing that we are the central character in our own life drama. This is because we have chosen, consciously or not, to focus our attention and concern on the people and events in the external world around us, rather than on our own internal state. Often, we can use absorption in the external world to avoid facing ourselves. Sometimes, indeed, we are so disconnected from soul that when we dare to look inside, we can sense only a terrifying black void. The external world can seem safer.

We can focus on pleasing others, or on controlling them, or on pleasures such as sex or food, or on amassing as much money as possible. When we choose to please others, such as our parents, children, work colleagues or friends, however, we place our worth in their hands and become dependent on their judgments. As we allow those judgments to influence us, we move further and further away from living from soul. We focus our concentration on their emotional wellbeing and disregard our own. We can negate the value of our own lives, and some of us might become so lost in pleasing others that we never carry out the work on ourselves that will lead us to see that the terrifying void within us is nothing more than an illusion, and that in its place actually lies the wonderful, peaceful contentment, self-love and compassion of our core soul being.

Unconditional Love – The Foundation of Life

It is innate to the nature of unconditional love to create and to nurture that which it creates. As human beings, it is in our nature to nurture everything that we create: our children, our friendships, our work, our lives and, of course, ourselves. The universe of which we are a part exists, expands and moves with an unimaginable creative force. If unconditional love is in essence creation, then creation is, in essence, unconditional love. It is true to say, therefore, that unconditional love informs everything that exists; it is everywhere. Without the unifying, creative influence of this love, our lives, our families, our societies, indeed our world would disintegrate into chaos.

At the beginning of the twenty-first century, our human world is still so full of war and political and social conflict that we might be forgiven for believing that love, let alone unconditional love, is a scarce commodity amongst humans. In fact, unconditional love is at work all the time, and evidence of its work can be found everywhere: from the way that people from across the world rush without question to help each other in times of disaster and crisis, to those small moments in every day when we ease the lives of those around us with a well-judged warm smile or a secret act of patience. The universal presence in our lives of the energy of unconditional love does not mean that our lives are perfect. Our lives are works in progress for which we are entirely responsible. As expressions of the pure creative force that animates us, however, we are also pure unconditional love, and the love that we experience, express and share in the world is no more and no less than a reflection of the pure love that we each are. In the game of living our lives, we learn more and more to let go of the fear that is so often our ego-mind's response to the circumstances that it experiences, and to drop down into, to exist and act from and to perceive in the world around us our innate nature of pure, unconditional love.

As human beings, we are social animals who instinctively wish to mate: to find a partner with whom to share our lives. Our natural tendency to express the love that we are is often conditioned by society into expressing itself in the form of searching for the romantic ideal: the one soul mate who perfectly mirrors who we are, who is our 'missing half', who completes us. The more we drop down into and live from our soul essence of unconditional love, however, the more liberated we become from such ideals. The more that we live from unconditional love as individuals, the more we work on ourselves, revealing and smoothing out the jagged, difficult, fearful aspects of our ego-minds using the tools of our deep self-compassion and patience. As we come to truly feel and express the love that we are, to love ourselves freely with acceptance and without judgment, we become more ready to love another in this way, and we will only attract and only be drawn to those who love themselves enough to recognise our kindred souls. So often our culture can reduce 'love' to conditional emotion, infatuation, sex and romance. Those experiences, however, are very small and temporary when compared to the profound, still, quiet, clear love and peace that we actually are. Sexual infatuation can be an all-consuming, thrillingly intense, often painful and frequently highly addictive energy, but it is not unconditional love. True lovemaking is an unconditional communion of soul to soul: a union of body, mind, heart and spirit.

Moving into living from a place of true love for ourselves and others is not a quick trick of the ego-mind. It requires our willingness to consistently and diligently address and release our fearful emotions, so that we can fill their place with love: pure love. This process is life-long, and its challenges, such as uprooting our oldest, deepest childhood fears of loneliness, dependency and abandonment, are difficult. We need all of our growing capacity for self-love, honesty and patience to complete this process. We also need the help of others, and they need our help. As each of us works on releasing our fears and moving into the expression of the pure, unconditional love that we are, we need to develop and to treat each other with perseverance, patience, gentleness and compassion, for all of us will slip many times.

As we practise being and expressing unconditional love, and releasing fear, we become more and more able to regard the world around us, and the events that affect us, with a tranquil objectivity. Each time that we encounter a frightening, stressful situation and choose to respond to it with love, instead of with our habitual fear, we have transmuted that fear into love. Even if we slip and experience that fear again, it will be lighter, more fleeting, because we will be able to adjust into love more quickly. As we come to live purely from soul, we come to be nothing less than pure expressions of the unconditional creative love that informs the world around us and everything within it.

Looking for Love Outside Ourselves

As discussed above, if we have not yet begun to explore and express our true soul nature of unconditional love, we will still be searching for love; we will still believe that love exists beyond ourselves. Dating websites are testimonies to the determination and energy that so many of us are willing to put into this search. In western society, our belief in the power of romantic love, indeed our belief that it is the most powerful, most real, most mountain-moving love of all, is fed by the innumerable cultural messages that we receive about it. Romantic love is everywhere that we look. Advertising agencies use it to sell products. Magazine pages are stuffed with tips on how to make ourselves thin enough, fashionable enough, witty enough, rich enough, sexually adept enough to attract and secure our mates. Interlaced between the tips are numerous articles on the happy or disastrous states of celebrity love lives.

Millions of pounds are spent on producing romantic comedies for the cinema and television. Our bookshops and libraries house millions of copies of romantic novels. We look for this love on the outside, because we do not yet know that the first place in which we need to find our real love is within ourselves. The less that we have found the love that we are, the more we will feel driven to look on the outside. The trouble is that the love inside us, the soul-level unconditional love that we are, is the only love that can truly fulfil us. There is no external substitute for this love. No one outside ourselves can meet our need for it, because they cannot recognise and do not know us as well as we can recognise and come to know and accept, and love, ourselves. Each of us needs to find our own love for ourselves before we are ready and able to truly love another.

Most of us reading this book are likely to have had one or more, or indeed many, romantic partners over the course of our lives. We might have entered into these partnerships with an honest and passionate commitment, being fully convinced that we would be parted only by death. When we are fully 'in love' with an external lover, we cannot believe that our love can end, that our lover could become a source of irritation, boredom, disappointment, pain or fear, but so often that is exactly what happens. When we fall romantically in love with someone, we place on them, and on ourselves, an extremely heavy burden. As said at the beginning of this book: so often, in romantic love, 'I love you' becomes 'and now you owe me happiness'.

If we love from the unconditional pure love that is our true self, however, our partnerships are not about owing, but about sharing our natural joy and happiness, our freely given love, care and attention. In these relationships, we are each responsible for our own happiness and we are each free to share our joy with the other; there is no seeking to control, no attachment, no wishing to be dependent, no demanding, no inequality, no imbalance, no shattering or erosion of romantic illusion, no boredom and disappointment. We do not take over the relationship, demanding that we be the centre of attention and that our lover be a mere helpmeet, living in constant acknowledgement of our need to grow and learn whilst ignoring his or her own needs. These relationships, rather, are simply and beautifully expressions of the delight, recognition and light of true unconditional love.

We are each, at root, an expression of unconditional love, and we are also the instrument through which that love flows. The deepening and growing of our experience, understanding and expression of the love that we are is a constantly evolving process of discovery. When truly loving ourselves, we are truly ready for love with someone else, and when we enter into partnerships with others we will find that the speed of our process of discovery quickens. We learn so much about ourselves, and about the requirements of being and expressing love, by observing ourselves in our relationships to the people whom we love and who love us. We gain, for example, a deeper understanding of patience, gentleness, acceptance, compassion and trust; we learn about the true communion of lovemaking; we learn about the need to balance our expression of the masculine and feminine aspects within ourselves.

We are love, and we express love, but it is in the nature of unconditional love to be free. When we love unconditionally, we give freedom to those whom we love. We do not own each other. Each partner comes to the other because each chooses to do so, and each will stay as long as that choice remains. When one, out of love for him or herself, makes the choice to change the relationship, for example from one of sexual engagement to one of friendship, unconditional love is expressed by the other in supporting and respecting the partner's freedom to make that change. Unconditional love does not know anger, jealousy or dependency, which arise from the fears of the ego-mind. It knows only freedom and gratitude for the wonderful love and learning that has been shared.

Peggy and Tom

Peggy attended a strict convent school from a very young age. At home, her parents never talked about sexuality, and she certainly never saw them naked. Both her mother and father believed that, like their sexuality, it was better and safer to repress, rather than express, their emotions, and they taught Peggy to do the same. Her parents were very strongly of the view that children should be seen but not heard. Peggy developed into a model daughter: the epitome of a 'good girl'. She always complied with her parents' wishes at home and with the nuns' instructions at the convent. By the age of ten, she was spending much of her free time baking cakes for people in the neighbourhood. By the age of 16, she was organising the food for weddings in her local community. Peggy grew up to be a shy, introverted and intelligent young woman who had excelled at her studies, both at the convent and later on at university.

Tom came from a working-class background. As a child, he spent a great deal of his time alone playing in the woods and fields near to his home. His parents were aloof, indeed almost cold, towards him, and preferred him to be out of their small flat so that they could spend quiet time together. If Tom interrupted their quiet time, his father would beat him soundly. Unsurprisingly, Tom became a very obedient son, who did everything that he could think of to earn the good opinion of his parents. He was adept at his school studies, and, although his parents failed to give him the praise and attention for this that he craved, he would listen in secret to his father showing off to their neighbours about his school achievements. This, of course, spurred Tom on to excel both at school and later on at university.

Peggy and Tom met during the course of their university studies, quickly fell in love and equally quickly decided to marry. In those first heady days of romance and sexual excitement, neither gave much thought to the baggage of childhood, emotional neglect and repression that each brought with them to the marriage. Soon after marrying, Peggy fell pregnant, and in a very short space of time she and Tom found themselves to be the proud, exhausted parents of a very young son and an even younger daughter.

As the children grew, Peggy and Tom's unresolved pain, fear and anger at their own parents' neglect began to surface. They began to have inexplicably angry fights with each other, and both often found themselves shouting impatiently at the children. Peggy and Tom each felt very guilty at these losses of their careful self-control, but they found themselves powerless to stop them. As time moved on, their marriage began to suffer from the arguments and from the fact that they never seemed to be able to find enough time to enjoy being with the children, with each other or even with themselves. Life seemed a constant struggle of long working hours overshadowed by fears of money shortages.

Peggy and Tom's love for each other, and for their children, was very strong. They were also both highly intelligent individuals, and as such they were able to sense that the hidden, destructive emotional patterns that each had developed in childhood were doing nothing to help their situation. They decided, therefore, to seek the help of a relationship counsellor. Over the course of three years with the counsellor, through much courageous, mutually compassionate and honest soul-searching, Peggy and Tom succeeded in bringing their hidden patterns into the open. Both were able to acknowledge and release their fear and anger at the lack of love, compassion and understanding that their parents had shown to them. Tom was able to understand and to forgive his father, and to let go of the rage and terror he had felt at the regular beatings he had received. Peggy and Tom both became able to overcome their longstanding sexual shyness and frustration. As soon as they became able to release their repressed emotions and fear, their marriage began to improve significantly.

The courage and wisdom to reveal, work with and release destructive forces within us comes from the unconditional love that we each are at the soul level. When we live from soul, we understand that for our own health and wellbeing and for that of those around us, especially those whom we love, we have to be able to express and live with the heat of our emotions. We do no good at all to ourselves or to others by suppressing our difficult feelings, because if we suppress them these feelings will simply erupt, often hurting the people whom we most love and most wish to protect. Unconditional self-love enables us to feel, express and release our emotions with gentleness, compassion and patience. We are always safe; the love that we are will always protect us. When we have the courage, self-love and faith to express truly who we are, the people who truly recognise and love us will not reject us. By being honest, we enable a true, unconditionally loving union with those with whom we share love. Furthermore, when we truly love and accept all the fearful aspects within ourselves, we can love these aspects in our partner.

Love and Sexuality

In some spiritual traditions, including some of the major religions, the divine is held to be separate from and superior to this physical world, and this has led to a rejection of the beauty of the communion in sensual, sexual love. Spiritual love is seen as pure and holy, something that must not be contaminated by sexual pleasure. Sex can be condoned solely for procreation: a necessary act, which, it can sometimes seem, must be completed as efficiently and joylessly as possible. If such traditions prevail, sexual feelings and acts can become sources of guilt and self-disgust. They can lead us to trying to distance ourselves from our instinctive need, as loving beings, to express intimacy at every level from soul to ego-mind to body, and from our body's natural, healthy capacity for delighting in its own sensual and sexual pleasure. Sex can become relegated to the soulless, unloving, isolating desperation of pornography. The unconditional love that we are at the core of our being, the 'divine' essence that we are, however, flows through nature and ourselves, and our natural, healthy sexual desire is no less than a pure expression of our divine love and of our need to express that love fully.

Our capacity and need for healthy sexual love can be abused, in pornography, for example, or when advertising uses lust to sell a thousand different products from car parts to Botox. Paedophilia and other psychosexual malfunctions are not innate evils, but are, rather, tragic expressions of the perpetuation of the abuse that we can inflict on ourselves and our children when we do not live from unconditionally loving soul, when our own innocence has been so abused and degraded that we have lost our way, have lost our connection to the pure love that we are.

The use of sexuality in advertising and the media is not a sign of a society or culture that is at peace with, let alone understands, the true joy, beauty and purity of sexual union between two loving adults. This use simply exploits the capacity of our ego-mind to be lured into lust. It reduces sexuality to little more than the scratching of an itch. When we engage in a sexual act with mutually open and loving hearts, we connect with each other at the deepest level, indeed on all levels. We express soul love; we connect as unconditionally loving souls. When we react from lust, however, when we use the other to live out our sexual fantasies, we are objectifying and merely using the person with whom we are having sex. We reduce sex to only one level: the body. Far from connecting us to the other, such an act only serves to isolate us even more in our own fear and loneliness.

Truly loving sexuality requires the courage of closeness, openness and selflessness. We do not use our sexual partner for our own pleasure, because our want is to provide them with profound pleasure, and our mutual desire is for us both to merge, through our bodies, minds and souls, into a spiritual communion in which our individual selves disappear. Maintaining feelings of pleasure and closeness needs truthful communication; we need to share feelings, thoughts and problems. Difficulties in relationships can arise when we cease to communicate on every level, and often, especially if we grew up in repressive or abusive households, communication on the level of sexual intimacy is the first to cease. How many couples lose sight of each other sexually, and then emotionally and spiritually, because they start hiding during the act of sex? If we lose the willingness to communicate, habit and boredom can set in, and it can be a short step, then, to using the body of the other to have sex with the different man or woman in our minds. Then there is guilt, fear, confusion and loneliness as both lovers begin instinctively to sense the separation, and it can be very hard to find our way back from that. When fear enters our sexual relationship, we cease to be able to express, accept and sustain pleasure easily.

The fulfilling expression of love through sexual pleasure requires our alertness, honesty and courage, for it is a delightful and intriguing game, a graceful dance, a clever and subtle exchange of energy, and we will never make love with two people, or with the same person on two occasions, in quite the same way. Sex is a river into which no man can step twice. It requires us to be aware in every moment and to act from and with our unconditionally loving soul. Physical love is not easy; pleasure and sexuality are individual to each person, and there is no universal recipe, but that is what makes physical love so exciting. When we are young, we might be impatient and unable to control the awakening force of physical love within ourselves. When we are old, our body might need more time and patience; the force of youth has gone, but there is now more inner peace and joy and more expertise. When we make love unconditionally from soul, it creates a connection with our partner that deeply intensifies our expression and experience of love. We are, each of us, love, and when we join together in the act of physical love we become a wonderful, joyous expression of love in motion.

Love and Emotion

When we love others unconditionally from soul, every part of us is involved: our soul, the thoughts and emotions of our ego-mind, and the sensuality of our body. When we love like this, we feel inspired, strong, courageous, free of all fear, and our imaginations and instincts are electrified; we feel truly alive. We can feel so connected to the person whom we love that it can feel as if they reside in our emotions, thoughts and bodies – inside our skin.

It is exhausting to sustain that degree of ecstasy, and those of us who grow wise in love, because we live and love unconditionally from soul, know that this 'electrification' is only the early part of loving another. As we grow to know the other, the flavour and character of our love changes, becomes softer, more gentle, less ecstatic, but deeper and warmer; it becomes more intimate, as we become more familiar with each other. When, however, we cling to the intensity of emotion experienced at the beginning of a relationship, that clinging can entrap us and cause us to refuse the natural progression of love. All relationships change constantly with time, and if we seek to hold on to what was, we will only stifle growth.

Equally, some of us, if we cannot yet love unconditionally from soul, can feel entrapped when our lover freely expresses their deepening love for us. The honesty and courage of that love can fill us with the fear that, if we stay, we will be bound to them, and be responsible for their emotional wellbeing, forever. How many of us, when expressing our deepening love for a lover, have heard them respond with a panicked 'but I'm not looking for a serious relationship', or 'I'm not old enough yet to have to settle down', or 'you should protect yourself from loving so much'? Often, a well-excused physical distancing will shortly follow such fearful remarks, and then we understand that the relationship is over. At the same time, of course, a relationship can run its course even if the one who ends it does love unconditionally. In a relationship we often come together for mutual learning and growth. Sometimes, one partner is following a direction the other one does not want to follow. Distance, life circumstances: there can be many reasons why we end relationships, not just because we cannot love unconditionally yet.

When we love unconditionally from soul, however, our love is not cowed by such reluctance. We learn, rather, wisdom from it, and understand that our two loves were out of kilter. We realise that we loved the other in a way for which they were not yet ready, and, because we love them purely and freely, we can wish them very well on their onward journey and let them go without pain or regret, but with gratitude and love for the experiences that we have shared with them and for the depth of love that we have felt in response to them. Their fear is a misunderstanding of unconditional love, which by its very nature is free and liberating because it cannot cling. We live with the illusion of separateness, when in reality there is only oneness. Loving unconditionally is an expression of oneness. Fear of loving is the feeling of separateness. When we accept our separateness, however, we accept our humanity, and in accepting our fear of separation we can work on it. Once we fill our own emptiness by learning to love ourselves unconditionally and to let go of fear, we can engage fully with a partner, as we no longer expect them to fill the void within us or to take us over. We have learnt that there is no void and that we are all equally free; we cannot be taken over.

As much as separateness is an illusion, so is the notion that we will ever know our partner completely. Soul energy is deep, and there is no limit to what it can reveal in ourselves and in our partner. If we grow lazy and settle down into a placid life together, ceasing to explore and discover each other, our love will feel stale, predictable and dull. This too is an illusion. When we love with the awareness, alertness and delight of soul, we can never take each other for granted. Exploring each other, we learn endlessly about each other, about ourselves and about what it is to be human. We keep the soul force of love alive when we connect with the soul of our partner. When we do this, we cannot experience life as a routine, and our attraction and connection to each other will stay alive.

Love and Friendship

The love of friendship can be as strong as that of sexual or emotional love, but can exist without them. Most of us will be lucky enough to have formed deep friendships in our lives with the few kindred spirits that we have encountered on our journey. Friendship is the love between equals, based on mutual respect, recognition and trust. It is one of the lasting pleasures of parenthood, for example, to grow into friendship with our children as they grow into adulthood.

It is also true to say that any relationship based on sexual and emotional love will not last if these are not accompanied by the love of friendship. Inherent within our love with our partner must be mutual recognition, respect and trust. We recognise our lover as the individual that they are, and we respect and accept every part of them, including the need that they will have for separateness: for space and solitude. Friendship is the location of peace, trust, respect and acceptance in any long-lasting sexual and emotional relationship.

Many years ago, when I began to practise as a healer, I belonged to a small healing circle led by a husband and wife couple, Jane and Sidney, who had been together for some years. One evening, whilst the group were discussing the nature of spiritual values, Jane announced without preamble that she was no longer interested in sexual love, because she had transcended it. She had become 'so spiritual' that she had transmuted all of her sexual desire into spiritual energy. All of our eyes fell helplessly on Sidney at that moment, who quietly looked away, embarrassed. We all felt embarrassment, too, but not for him; to all of us it felt, rather, as if Jane were operating from a profoundly mistaken perception of life and the place of spirituality within it.

There is no separation or hierarchy in love. When all aspects of love come together, we are truly blessed. Relating to our partner sexually and emotionally, and as a friend, we journey together through the joys and challenges of life. From those joys and challenges, and from the ways in which we individually react to them, we deepen our understanding of love and of life; we come to live more and more from our unconditionally loving soul perspective. If we choose to withdraw from the loving intimacy of our bodies' connection, we stop our love progressing and deepening, and when this happens we stop progress in our lives together. Our relationship begins to stagnate, and can so easily turn into distance and resentment.

There are many 'spiritual' concepts in existence that state that we can only achieve true inner peace if we do not indulge in sexual and emotional interaction. Such concepts, however, express a profound error of understanding, for such denial is simply a denial of the true nature of life and can lead only to an illusion of inner peace, not to the reality of enlightened unconditional soul love itself. What can inner peace mean, if we have to withdraw from, protect ourselves from a fully lived and loving life in order to experience it?

Soul Mates

Through the myths and stories and spiritual teachings that we have encountered in our societies, religions and cultures, many of us have come to believe that somewhere out there exists our true soul mate, quietly waiting for us. If we have already experienced the wonder of a truly open, committed and unconditionally loving relationship, the chances are that we have already encountered a soul mate, but how do we recognise one when we meet him or her for the first time?

Our ideal of a soul mate is of someone with whom we feel an instant and deep affinity, a profound recognition, an instant connection. They are someone who deeply recognises us for who we are on a soul level. When we meet them, they seem strangely familiar, as if we have known them for years. It does not necessarily matter what gender they are, or what direction our own sexual orientation takes. Soul mates are kindred spirits; who they are matters far more than what they are. Soul mates accept and embrace us with unconditional love. Once we meet them, even if we become physically parted through death, they never leave us; we let them into the deepest, purest part of our being. They reside peacefully in our souls. To love and be loved by a soul mate is a profoundly beautiful experience. It is one of the purest expressions of the creative force of unconditional love that we are at the deepest level of soul.

It would be a mistake, however, to assume that the day-to-day experience of a soul mate relationship is a perpetually blissful, harmonious pursuit of an ideal shared purpose. Not at all, thank goodness!

Yes, there is the wonder of that deep recognition, but it can be accompanied by much disagreement, complexity and confusion. I have a friend who met a soul mate at work and agreed to marry him on their first date. She described to me how the moment came when they were paddling in the sea off Brighton Pier, having just posted their banns, and they both looked at each other with total shock and surprise, wondering what on earth they were doing! They did marry, had two children, and then, within three years of their wedding, he became terminally ill with cancer. In the four years that remained to them before he died, they and their children learnt some of the most beautiful, profound and difficult lessons about what it is to love and to be human.

My friend has been a single parent, living quietly on her own with her children in a messy old house that she never has time to tidy, for the last 11 years. If I were to ask her now if she regretted the difficulties, pain and sorrow of those last four years, she would say 'not at all', because the laughter, the honesty, the warmth, and the strength and beauty of the unconditional love that passed between herself, her husband and their children during those years was a privilege and a blessing: one of the most powerful, meaningful and enlightening experiences of all of their lives.

Soul mates do not 'complete' by the fact of their existence in our lives. Each soul mate, rather, helps the other to grow and to learn, and to live more and more from the unconditional love of soul. Soul mates do not complete us; they help us to complete ourselves.

Spiritual Love

When we experience spiritual love in response to another person, we are experiencing pure, unconditional soul-to-soul love: a far deeper response than our attraction to the other's intellect, emotional nature and physical body. Spiritual love is full of soul, purely full of soul; it is true soulful love. When we love at this level we recognise and embrace what is completely unique within the other person: the beauty of his or her soul. When we connect with our partner spiritually, we experience their true individuality.

As we develop the habit of living from our own soul, of loving ourselves unconditionally with compassion and acceptance and trust, we become able to recognise the soul in others and to love them in the same way. We connect with them at the soul level, and in this connection there is a total liberation from fear; only a pure, quiet recognition, respect and peace remains. We each remain separate entities, but through each other we glimpse the oneness of which we are all a part.

Spiritual, soulful love is not affected by the ebb and flow of the sexual, emotional and intellectual energies between lovers. Spiritual love is also not confined to lovers; rather, it is the deep, quiet unconditional love that we can feel for those whom we most deeply love, respect and trust. Such people might be friends, parents, children, teachers or colleagues; we recognise and know them by our spiritual response to them.

Spiritual, unconditional loving from soul does not mean that there will not be times when we experience dissonance in our relationships with the people whom we love. Of course not! Life is a dance between human and soulful aspects. Love, at all levels, sometimes makes us learn through challenge and difficulty. Our daily living can sometimes feel like a constant negotiation between the wisdom of our soul, asking us to seek oneness, and the urges of our ego-mind and body to disconnect and rest in separateness. We can love a partner unconditionally from soul, but still sometimes feel a very human hurt, confusion and anger at their behaviour to us if they are unexpectedly thoughtless, distant or selfish.

Loving each other is a day-to-day work in progress at both the soul and human levels of our being, but there is much mutual joy, delight and enlightenment to be had in that work. It is work that is always worthwhile, not just because learning to love and live with another person helps us to learn about and love ourselves, but also because it is only by taking the risk, and having the courage, to open ourselves to loving another person and to being loved by them that we can truly experience and explore the nature of oneness, the creative, loving energy that binds together and interconnects all there is.

Love in the World

As we grow increasingly able to live from soul, and to love and understand ourselves and others unconditionally and clearly, that clear and wise love flows out beyond us and into the world. It must do so, because by its very nature love is creative, energising, ever-expanding; it is the very essence of who we are.

Unconditional soulful love is the giving of love, the being of love, without any expectation of return. Love that is a true expression of soul is felt through its effects, and any expression of this love, whether large or small, has the same value. For each of us, in every single one of our days, there are countless ways in which we can express that love: the spontaneous embrace of loving warmth, forgiveness and reconnection that comes between two people, be they lovers, friends or parent and child, after an argument; the instant letting go of anger when the driver of another car selfishly refuses to honour our right of way; the acknowledgement and grateful smile that we give to an overworked cashier in a supermarket; our unquestioning willingness to give what we have, be it our money, time or physical resources, to those across the world who are in crisis; our unwavering commitment to our active participation in the creation of a wiser, saner, fairer and more loving human world, which will live in peace and harmony with the Earth and the flora and fauna that inhabit it.

Soulful Living and Raising Our Children

When we live from and express the unconditional love of soul, as we practise living from this deepest place within us, as we learn to realign ourselves with it every time we slip, we begin to become good role models for our children. The best example that we can present to our children is to love ourselves with compassion and patience, and to love them in the same way. What our children need most from us is our openness, our honesty, and our unconditional love, recognition and acceptance of them. They need our clear guidance and our provision of clear boundaries. They also need to know that we are enthralled by and celebrate their uniqueness: the ways in which they are beginning to express and find themselves in the world. We must teach our children, too, to know that it is all right, it is safe, to make mistakes, because there is so much learning in each mistake; the making of mistakes is how we acquire wisdom. Being a parent is one of the most wonderful gifts that we can experience in life, and it is also a powerful and sometimes daunting responsibility. All we can do is do our best, and the best that we can do is to operate as a parent with the wisdom, compassion, acceptance and strength of our unconditional love in every moment that we can.

Through what we say and do, and how we say and do it, we influence all of the children with whom we come into contact: our own, those of friends and colleagues, our children's friends from school, the children whom we might teach either through our profession or in our work for voluntary groups. Who children become as adults, and how they come to treat each other and the world around them, will depend very largely on how they are treated by us. In our work on ourselves in learning to live more and more from soul, we are already seeking to improve our human relationship with the world. The children whom we influence, if we influence them well, will carry on that improvement.

Children do not need perfection from us; often they are far more naturally compassionate and gentle in their judgments than we have learnt to be. They are busy becoming, and as adults we are also busy becoming, but for us that becoming involves a lot of undoing: of releasing the fear-based reactions that we learnt to adopt in our own childhoods. Children do not need us to be perfect; they need only to see and feel our intention to encounter life with enthusiasm and unconditional love. They need most of all to know that we love them and recognise them as the precious expressions of creative, loving energy, the incredible potential that they are.

Children are not an alien race, nor are they automatons to be seen and not heard, nor are they innately manipulative or 'bad'. They are small, young people learning their way in the world, and they deserve to be treated with the respect that we would give unhesitatingly to another adult. To a large extent they are *tabula rasa*; what we do with them will help to write their conditioned responses to the world. If our own upbringing was poor, we might sometimes need expert, patient loving help to develop our own healthy emotional responses to our children, so that we can freely feel and express towards them unconditional love and commitment, acceptance, patience, celebration, enthusiasm and trust. We might also need help in developing vital parenting skills, such as the important skill of talking and listening effectively with children, and that of creating clear, fair rules and boundaries, which children can understand and are happy to honour.

Physical Nurturing

From the moment that we choose to conceive a child to the moment that our child begins to leave our care as a young adult, we take on the responsibility for ensuring that, in every moment of the incredible development of this new child's body and mind, we are working with the alertness of our soul awareness to ensure that everything that we do, feel and think and everything that we put into our bodies will help them to thrive, and will certainly do them no harm. Having a child should never be a thoughtless act, but a considered, unconditionally loving one. Yes, sometimes conception begins when we cannot complete the process, and sometimes, in those incredibly difficult situations, we might, out of unconditional love for ourselves, come to the grave decision that the most loving act of all, for both mother and the potential life within her, is to terminate the pregnancy. When conception occurs through the anger, violence and hatred of rape, for example, it can be impossible for a woman to find within herself the capacity to give birth to the offspring of such an act.

Fortunately, most of us will never be faced with such a terrible choice. For us, there is the simple ensuring that as expectant mothers we consume the right healthy food and vitamins; that we sleep well; that we do not smoke cigarettes or take unnecessary drugs, including alcohol; that we keep our bodies as toned and fit as possible. Once our children are born, we ensure, equally, that we can provide them with healthy, nutritious breast milk, and as they grow we ensure that all the food that we give them is as fresh and healthy and balanced as possible. By nurturing our children's bodies, we are doing the best that we can to help their bodies and minds to develop fully. A physically weak child is prone to illness, and under-nourishment in childhood can lead to significant health deficiencies as an adult. In our rich western society of fast food, overindulgence and rising childhood obesity, providing our children with healthy food is of utmost importance. It is also our responsibility to provide them with fresh air, exercise and stimulation, and to help them to look after their own health by such simple acts as washing their hands after using the toilet. In nurturing our children's bodies and helping them to nurture their own bodies, we express unconditional, wise soul love for them.

Emotional Nurturing

As vulnerable, defenceless children, nothing is more important to us than being able to trust the parents whom we naturally love, and to know that they love us unconditionally and express that love in everything that they do with us. Just as babies need the reassurance of loving physical closeness, so too do children as they grow. Children need the reassurance of closeness, cuddling and laughter; of being told 'we love you' repeatedly.

Children also need to be able to live in a harmonious, loving environment in which they feel safe. Children sense very acutely, and are acutely distressed by, discord between parents, which if it is continuous can have severe and lasting effects; it teaches children to live in fear and to stifle their own distress, because they know that their parents already cannot cope. Children have the need and right to be children. They are not responsible for parenting and protecting their own parents.

Parenthood can be exhausting, and while mothers and fathers will invariably disagree and argue from time to time, such disharmony should not be allowed to linger unresolved. One of the key responsibilities that we have as soul-conscious parents is to show our children that disagreements are a natural part of expressing who we are, and that it is safe to disagree. We show this by ensuring that every argument is followed swiftly by an expression of love and forgiveness in the form of mutual apology and a warm physical embrace.

Unconditional soulful love is the giving of love, the being of love, without any expectation of return. When we choose to be parents, we choose to bring this love into our parenting. A happy, stimulating home environment; committed and loving parental attention; the consistent expression and instilling of positive attitudes, thoughts, values and beliefs will all help our children to be healthy, happy, loving and fulfilled within themselves, and to make loving, healthy contributions to the world as they move into it. When we, as parents, show love towards family, society and humanity, so will our children.

Spiritual Nurturing

What is the difference, if any, between a religious and a spiritual upbringing? A religious faith will convey and teach important spiritual values such as the need to live our lives with honesty, integrity, selflessness and love. A religious faith also, however, requires us to accept and follow a certain set of beliefs. Some religions can be more relaxed than others in allowing their adherents to explore the value of the beliefs that their doctrines espouse. Other religions are less tolerant, and many people have lived lives consumed by a crippling guilt triggered by the sin of daring to act against the beliefs of their faith. As innocent, impressionable beings, children are very vulnerable to the influences of religious faith, including the capacity of that faith to lay the seeds of guilt.

As children, however, we are naturally closer to our spiritual centre, to our 'divine' unconditionally and spontaneously loving soul self, because we have not yet developed the complexity of intellectual and emotional response to life that afflicts a typical adult. If we love our children unconditionally from soul, we are wise enough to let them discover their own spiritual path, to reach their own conclusions. No religion is necessary. When we live from soul, our children can be guided by our example of what it is to live and be unconditional creative love.

When we, by example and through talking and exploring with our children as equals, begin to show our children how to live from soul, begin to help them to understand how they can centre themselves within the powerful expression of unconditional creative love that they are, begin to help them to sense their oneness with everything around them and gain the respect for everything around them that this engenders, we are helping our children to begin their own spiritual journey in life. When children are granted the respect and freedom to do this, they will find their own way to their divine centre. They will discover who they truly are. As they do so, they will cease to be afraid of becoming adults but will be eager to reach out and explore the world, knowing that their true home, to which they can return at any time that they choose and in which, indeed, they can choose to live in every moment, lies within them, at their unconditionally loving soul core.

The tenets of a religion are normally expressions of the spiritual experience of someone else, often someone who lived thousands of years ago. This spiritual experience is passed down through the generations and, with time, becomes the tenets, the doctrinal beliefs, to which followers of the religion are expected to adhere. Religion can, of course, help people who are searching for their own spiritual home; they can find their own profound spiritual experiences through it. If a child, as she or he moves towards adulthood, comes to choose a particular religious faith as the safest path home, or chooses to create his or her own unique path, this will be his or her choice, freely made, and whatever is chosen will be a perfect choice made by that child for that child.

Role Models

Children intuitively open towards anything that shows them the beauty and meaning of life. Accordingly, in the ways in which we express our unconditional love and commitment to them, and in the ways in which we teach them, by example and through discussion, about the values of love, integrity, service, acceptance, trust, compassion and peace, we help them to discover and instil within themselves a higher sense of purpose, the ability and the inner resources to live in a loving, helpful way.

Children are gentle, sincere and compassionate by nature. They look towards their parents for a personal example to follow, as well as to their friends, teachers and neighbours. They are also influenced, negatively or positively, by a plethora of other powerful sources: television, blockbuster films, magazines, the internet, mobile phone applications, interactive game platforms, books, the lyrics of their favourite pop songs, etc., etc. Many of these can exert a hypnotic pull on our children's attention; only recently reported in the press was the death of an overweight young man, who died from an unsuspected thrombosis believed to have been caused by his habit of sitting playing on his games console for 12 hours a day. As loving parents it is our responsibility to guide our children wisely when we can see them being drawn into such addictive behaviour.

This is an example of what it is like to be a good role model: as parents, we need to be able to say no, to impose time limits and sanctions, even if this makes us the most unpopular person in our household! It is especially important to prevent our children from over-exposure to films, games, websites, television programmes, books and music that indulge in, and at the same time trivialise, excessive emotional, verbal and/or physical violence and abuse. If our children become desensitised to such ugliness through their over-exposure to it, they will find it dangerously easy to adopt that behaviour themselves. If they are allowed to do so, we can only hold ourselves responsible.

As parents, we have the tremendous responsibility of being by far the most important role models for our children. Contemporary family life, with both parents often working outside the home and with children often participating in many activities outside school, is so hectic in pace, however, that it can be very difficult to find meaningful, quiet, uninterrupted time to be with our children. This lack is so endemic in western society that there can be little wonder at our children's tendency to resort to other, unhealthy activities to prevent themselves from feeling lonely and ignored. As busy parents, how many of us could honestly say that we have never used the television to 'babysit' our children while we have been attending to some urgent adult task?

When we live lovingly from soul, we find the determination to find the right time, and ample amounts of the right time, to be with our children. Often, organised daily family meal times, such as breakfast or, even better, dinner, can prove the best locations for such moments. As loving parents, we also need to give our children other fixed routines. Weekly family activities such as swimming outings or visits to the library give us valuable opportunities to spend enjoyable time with our children, finding out about who they are, who they see themselves to be, what is happening in their lives and what they think about the world: their excitement or fear or confusion about it. From when they can first begin to articulate their thoughts, children love discussions and delight in expressing and furthering their understanding of the world.

As loving parents, we all have to encourage our children to move away from us and out into the world as they become ready. We will always be here to love and support them, but we need to let them go, because they need to discover fully who they are and to make their own loving contributions to the world around them; they need to begin actively helping to create the world in which they choose consciously to live.

Our children do not ever owe us any debt of staying at home to be responsible for us. If we have done our best to love our children in every moment, unconditionally from soul, it is reward enough to know that they will take into the world all of the knowledge and skills that we have encouraged and helped them to acquire. These include the tools to lead a joyful life, the wisdom to develop their own spiritual foundation, the innate knowledge that they are always free to make their own choices.

Raising a child is the most responsible task for a human being, and one of the hardest, but it is also one of the most exhilarating and satisfying. Most of us receive no formal training at all for the job of producing the next generation. All we can do is try to operate from our unconditionally loving soul centre and to apply, healthily, our own wisdom and the knowledge that has come to us from our own upbringing. Sometimes, this means that we consciously avoid the mistakes of our parents, but in so doing move too far the other way and indulge our own children too much. Sometimes, it means that we find ourselves, suddenly, unconsciously repeating the very behaviour of our parents that we swore to ourselves as children we would never repeat. How many of us have found the nagging voice of our own mother springing forth from our mouths, or her admonishing finger sternly wagging our own? All we can do, in loving ourselves, is laugh at these momentary slips and readjust. If our children see us doing so, they will be more gently amused than horrified when they find themselves doing it too with their own children.

In each generation, all we can do is try to live from soul and to be the best parent that we can be. If our family histories are littered with tales of bad parenting, fear, neglect and violence, all we can do in each subsequent generation is seek to break the cycle of dysfunction through our conscious effort and our loving diligence, and that is good enough.

Discipline

A few words here about discipline: if we lack consistency in the treatment of our children – if we are, for example, sometimes too lax, or sometimes too strict, in imposing the agreed rules – we will create confusion, fear and worry in our children, and they will seek to test us to find out where the limits actually lie. We need to be consistent for their sake. This does not, however, cancel out the other difficult part of a parent's job in creating discipline, which is to know which battles to choose: to know when to impose the rules strictly and when to let them go. If our daughter has just been 'dumped' by her first boyfriend, flies into our kitchen in wails and tears, and fails to be polite to the local dignitary taking tea with us, it is not the time to punish her for rudeness. It is the time to take her quietly but firmly by the hand out of the kitchen and into the living room, to hold her in our arms, and to pour our unconditional love, acceptance and commitment into her. Anyone worthy of the post of local dignitary will understand!

Communication

Effective interactive communication with our children is such an important part of soul-based parenting that it is imperative for us to do it well. If, as parents, we express our feelings freely and easily, our children will feel able to express their own feelings in the same way. This does not mean that everyone resorts to shouting, but that each family member expresses his or her feelings with respect and gentleness: an art in itself that we would all do well to learn!

Furthermore, if we ask questions and offer explanations, so will our children. If we think out loud, so will our children. If, as children, we learn to discuss problems, the future adult that we will become will also feel confident in discussing problems with family, friends and colleagues. If, as parents, we show our children how to weigh up different options in terms of their respective likely consequences, we will teach our children to think in the same helpfully structured way.

If we respect ourselves and our children, they will respect themselves and others. Children have the right to be taken seriously, and to be treated with respect and tenderness. They have their own thoughts, emotions and dreams. When we respect them, they will feel good about themselves and will respect us in turn. As parents, we need to be an uplifting example to our children, and we can do this most easily when we approach them from unconditional soul love. Our thoughts about life will influence our children just as much as our actions, and we need to make every effort, therefore, to live in and from the wisdom, compassion, acceptance and patience inherent within our soul consciousness.

One of the key lessons that we need to teach our children is to take responsibility for, to own fully, their behaviour, choices and decisions in life. There is no value in the victimhood that inexorably grows from learning to blame everyone else: other family members, ex-lovers, employers, politicians, our society, our culture, our social class etc. We alone are responsible for living our lives honestly and lovingly from soul, and we need to help our children, too, to understand the liberating power of taking responsibility for themselves and their lives.

More on the Natural Spirituality of Children

It is inherent to the nature of all human beings to be born with a mind and heart that is open, curious and non-judgmental. As previously discussed, children come into the world strongly connected to the unconditionally loving creative force at the core of their being. They have an innate sense of connection, of oneness, with every other created thing around them. They will learn their judgments from us, and so we must choose very carefully which judgments, if any, we express in front of them. Indeed, we have here a wonderful opportunity to learn from our children: to use their example to rediscover our own innate capacity for acceptance, for being non-judgmental. One of the eternal delights of being a parent is indeed that of learning by observing our children. By being careful in what we express, we can also help them to preserve their instinctive joy and clarity, and in so doing we help them to nurture within themselves the confident, innate knowing that they can lead joyful and fulfilled lives.

In us, children see what it is like to be an adult, and part of the way in which they learn is by mimicking us. They will learn our habits, our tone of voice and our expressions, and, unless we have the vigilance and self-awareness that comes with soul loving, they might also adopt our unconsciously expressed limiting beliefs about life. Children take their cue from us; when we enjoy the wonders of the world, they will share our enchantment. They will share our delight: at playing tennis in the garden in the middle of a thunderstorm, at running into the sea madly to catch the ends of a double rainbow, at watching the vast red disc of the evening sun slip silently below the horizon, at standing in awestruck wonder at the capacity of the harvest moon to remain suspended in an infinite night sky. In each interaction with our children, in each shared experience, we have the opportunity to support and foster their sense of wonder at the world, their excitement at being alive in it, and their positive sense of themselves as wonderful, loving and loved beings of huge creative potential. We do this with words of acceptance, love and encouragement, and by asking them for their thoughts, opinions and questions, listening to them and answering them with respect and focus.

The unconditional, creative love for life is not something that we need to instil in our children, because it already resides in the core of their soul being. As parents, it is our responsibility to nurture that soul sense, to value it and to allow it to have a voice. We ourselves benefit from and are renewed by this process; when we spend time with a child who is expressing their deep curiosity and vast imagination about the world, these qualities are renewed within ourselves. The innocent questions that children ask us can also liberate us from our entrenched thinking about the world. Children have insights and experiences that give them a wonderful certainty regarding their nature, morality and spirituality. As adults, we can know everything that there is to know about the arcane subjects of nutrition, psychology and educational techniques. We are efficient and responsible in organising and ordering our children's lives, transporting them from lessons to clubs to games practices to social events, buying their clothes and uniforms, monitoring their homework etc., etc. They, however, in their natural innocent sense of wonder and in their deep innate connection to the unconditional soul love that they are, have so much to teach us.

Can we help our children to nurture and develop their instinctive spirituality so that it stays with them throughout their lives: so that they never lose it to fear, and so never have to find it again? Let us consider the example of the spiritual teaching offered by schools like the Huntington School in York. This school has as a part of its ethos the belief that its teachers owe a responsibility to their students to help them to develop their spirituality. The school's mission is to develop a sense of awe and wonder in its pupils for all that is good in life. It wants its pupils to nurture a sense of transcendence, to find a purpose within, and a deeper knowledge about, themselves. The school believes that such nurturing will help the moral, social and cultural development of the children within its care. In supporting the spiritual consciousness of the pupils, it is helping the children to relate to the world in a consistently loving way.

The students have left comments about their education on the school's website. Sarah Birkinshaw, who joined the Huntington School sixth form after taking her GCSEs in Leeds, commented thus: 'I chose to come to Huntington School because of the positive atmosphere which is constantly being generated here. We are constantly being encouraged to try new experiences and to take on more responsibility: a vital quality needed for the adult world. Sixth Formers run two key aspects of the Sixth Form calendar: Charity Week, where we are given the chance to organise and run projects, and the Pantomime, which is written and performed exclusively by ourselves. I really appreciate the respect the teachers give us in return.'

The Value of Time Spent in Nature

Some of the key ways in which we, as parents, can nurture our children's spirituality within our home environment are by helping them to expand their imaginations, encouraging their dreams and celebrating their achievements. One of the easiest and most mutually beneficial ways is to help them from their earliest years to develop a strong relationship with nature. Kindness, compassion, patience, trust, an understanding of the birth and death inherent in the cycle of physical life, a sense of connectedness to all things and a sense of awe at the profound, multifaceted beauty of the natural world: these will all grow in our children as they develop their relationship with nature.

There are so many ways in which we can foster this relationship: by taking our children for walks on the seashore, collecting sea glass and asking them to help us to identify the sea shells on the beach and the clouds in the sky; strolling with them over the cliffs and downs and through forests, asking them to help us to identify the trees and shrubs and the birds and insects that we come across;

encouraging them to create their own flower plots in our back gardens at home; allowing them to keep and be responsible for pets – from dogs to gerbils, or even spiders, depending on the room we have available. Through our walks through nature we can help our children to become aware of the nature of the changing seasons. We can also do this by building bonfires to celebrate each equinox and solstice, the first fall of snow in winter or the first budding crocus in spring.

From our connection with nature, there is only a small step to our connection to everything. When our children begin to develop such a sense of connection, a feeling of responsibility and service to others is a natural next step. Indeed, many schools here and in America incorporate community service and charity work into the key parts of their curricula.

Valuing Our Children's Thoughts

How do we normally listen to what our children have to say? Is it always from our unconditionally loving soul centre? Is it always with our full care and attention? A dear friend of mine, Janice, clearly remembers an animated family conversation about the purpose of life held with her parents and siblings when she was about ten years old. Janice remembers listening very politely and patiently to the contributions of all the other participants, before quietly announcing, 'I know what my purpose of life is: it is to live my life to the best of my abilities.' Her parents were in awe of the fact that such a profound statement could come from a child of such a tender age, but it showed them clearly that children can deeply and instinctively feel their essential soul nature. To the present day, Janice has followed the dictum that she announced that long-ago afternoon. It was then, and it still is, such a profound expression of who she is that she has always been able to follow it with a natural ease and peace.

One of the hardest tasks that we can set ourselves is trying to find the words to express the insights that flood into us when we live from and express the unconditional love of soul. As we have said previously in this book, human language is such a clumsy tool with which to express an insight, an instinctive sense that is both quintessentially simple and infinitely profound. If we do not try to articulate our insights, however, and if we fail to hear and honour our children's attempts to express theirs, our children might come, out of a fear of ridicule, to limit themselves: guarding and suppressing their feelings and understandings.

We are also beholden as parents to encourage in our children a sense of deep gratitude and awe at the opportunity that they have been granted to be alive in this world, at this time and in this place. A friend of mine's family has a daily ritual for just such a purpose. Each evening, mother and father and their three children sit together at the children's bedtime to tell each other why they have been grateful for the passing day, what they regret doing or failing to do in that day, and what they intend to do the next day. This ritual enables the sharing of joys and frustrations, and inspires in all participants a joyful gratitude for life.

Valuing Our Children's Imagination

In adulthood, our imagination, ability to visualise and capacity to dream provide us with vital tools to help us to drop down into, and practise living from, the unconditional love that we are at the soul core of our being. Our children are born into the world living naturally and effortlessly from the still centres of their souls, and they also bring with them an innate capacity for joy, a profound curiosity, and a wonderfully inventive and tireless imagination. Childhood is a time for endless exploration of the world: not just the physical world around us, but the infinite, magical world that we can visit in our minds by using our imagination to place ourselves in the middle of thrilling stories, stuffed with incredible characters and taking place in fantastical countries in whatever extraordinary past or future time we care to choose. When we celebrate our children's imagination, we confirm their knowledge that life is something exciting and rich. If we can provide tools to aid their imaginative leaps – dressing-up trunks full of mysterious old clothes; a plentiful supply of colourful fairy tale, travel and history books; a tent or tree house at the end of the garden; a family habit of making up exciting, scary and/or comic stories with which to entertain each other – we are doing much to help them to develop their imaginations, their sense of adventure, their ability to experience and articulate different thoughts and feelings, and their confidence in their abilities to grasp and negotiate the world. Often, particularly in times of stress, children can also develop imaginary friends to help them cope. As parents, we need to accept these temporary friends rather than be frightened by them; they will fade away naturally when our children no longer need them.

Valuing Our Children's Dreams

It is also very important that, as parents, we fully support our children in achieving their dreams. We should feel blessed when our children feel safe enough in our love to tell us what they most want to achieve in the world as they grow up. I have a friend whose young daughter wishes only to spend her adult life singing and acting at the top London theatres, and whose young son dreams only of playing for one of the most successful English Football League clubs. The dreams of both children lie in areas where there are enormously high levels of competition; while not impossible, it is improbable that they can achieve their dreams, but how will they know if they can achieve them if they do not try?

My friend's philosophy, therefore, is to think that there is no reason why her son and daughter might not achieve the improbable. She is a firm believer in the tactic of 'taking the leap of faith, knowing that the net will appear'. She works with her children every day to instil in them the knowledge that raw talent on its own will not be enough to achieve their dreams. They also need to work hard in every possible moment to hone their talents into skills, and they must be willing and courageous enough to focus on what they want and to stick with it. It is widely acknowledged that it takes one thousand hours to make a world-class expert in any field: one thousand hours, total focus, some raw talent, a lot of determination and, of course, a little luck. If we want our children to achieve their dreams, we need to acknowledge and support them. Children develop a vitally important 'it-can-be-done' attitude when we do so; they learn to value their dreams, to develop self-confidence, persistence and tenacity, and to pick themselves up after setbacks.

The Value of Ritual

Children can take great delight in simple rituals such as the blessing of our food before we eat, the burning of sage sticks throughout our home to clear out stale energy as the seasons change, or the lighting of candles to concentrate and send our good wishes to loved ones who are in distress. In some family households, a corner is also set aside for a quiet place, often with an altar, where family members can come when they need to sit in contemplation or meditation. Such things help children to be mindful and to develop their spiritual sense.

A Little More About Nurturing Spirituality

For the many of us who follow a particular religious faith, we will nurture our children's natural spirituality within our faith community. Such a community can give the whole family the support of like-minded others, a clear structure and a sacred space within which to share, celebrate, explore, clarify and develop our spiritual beliefs. Spiritual gatherings also often provide children with the invaluable experience of mixing with people from different ethnic and cultural backgrounds, and from different generations.

Those of us who do not subscribe to an organised religion, but who have a 'secular' spirituality based on our internal connection to the unconditionally loving essence of soul at the core of our being, are also likely to have communities of like-minded friends and colleagues to which we can introduce our children for the same purpose of helping them to experience and explore their spirituality. We can also work with our children to help them to sense their connectedness to and oneness with all things so that they can nurture a healthy, loving respect for all living and non-living things. We can use words and examples that our children can understand. We can talk to them in simple terms, using simple comparisons and metaphors, about the indestructible nature of energy, about the ideas that are pouring forth from contemporary astrophysics on the origin, nature and composition of the universe, and about the ideas associated with quantum physics regarding the possibility that our thoughts can energetically influence the subject of our attention.

Love Is Always Stronger than Fear

We interact with our children constantly, and every time that we do so our children, either subtly or sharply, are changed by that interaction. We must, as parents, therefore, be diligent and watchful over the ways in which we respond to our children's thoughts, feelings and actions. It is all too easy to develop a habit of expectation, and consequent expression, that prevents us from being totally present in the current moment, so that we are not responding to what our children are actually saying or doing but to what we have come to want them to say or do, or to fear that they are saying or doing. If we always feed our children negative impressions of themselves – that they are, for example, difficult, lazy, rude, fat, naughty, awkward or ungrateful – they will tend to act out those expectations. They will also become more and more distant from us, because they will feel, rightly, that we can no longer see them. They will feel unnoticed, and ultimately unloved, by us. If we make the equal mistake of telling them constantly that they are, for example, beautiful, clever, special or perfect, they will again feel that we cannot really see them. Our positive comments may be well meant, but they are setting up impossible expectations for our children to meet. No one can be beautiful, clever and perfect all the time!

If, instead, we seek to respond freshly and accurately, with compassion, patience and unconditional love, to our children's actions in each moment, we will help them to understand truly who they are in each moment. Also, it is imperative upon us to remember the one sacrosanct rule: that we never criticise our children themselves, only their behaviour.

In the heat of a stressful moment, we are bound to slip: to hurl impatience, anger or disappointment directly at our children for something that, should they have done it at any other time, we might have let go or even laughed at. This is okay. If our children know us to be the unconditionally loving, open and honest parents that we are, our momentary exasperation will not cause them to withdraw from us in fear and confusion. They love us as unconditionally as we love them, and our outburst will teach them something profoundly important about what it is to be an adult and a parent: that we are human and fallible, that we can make mistakes, overreact, just as much as they do. Our reaction will also make them think about the behaviour of theirs that caused it, and lead to an adjustment in their future behaviour; they will become more thoughtful and more considerate, more aware of the signs that we are experiencing stress.

In these situations, the most important corrective action that we can take as loving parents is simply to say sorry, to offer a warm embrace, to explain our slip, to sit with our children for a while and reconnect with loving warmth and laughter. When love is present, forgiveness is easy.

We can be so determined to be 'perfect' parents that our slips can cause us to carry a heavy burden of guilt. This is both unnecessary and unhelpful. It is better not to try for the illusion of perfection, but simply to try to be unconditionally loving in every moment that we can be, to have compassion for ourselves when we slip, and to seek to learn from that slip so that we can act more calmly next time. We do not have to be perfect, which is impossible. We simply have to be loving to ourselves and to our children, and be willing to try a different response: perhaps next time we could stop and take a deep breath before we react.

Mark

My colleague, Mark, told me often about how wonderfully loving and patient his father and mother had been. When he and his brothers and sisters were young, Mark's mother would encourage them every evening to rush out to greet their father with warmth and hugs as soon as his car had pulled up in their driveway. Mark would fight good-naturedly with his siblings over who would have the honour of carrying their father's briefcase and newspaper into the house.

Mark had an idealised memory of his father, who was never too tired to play with the children, even after a punishing long day at work. His father also constantly encouraged his children in all their endeavours and always praised their efforts. He was, in Mark's memory, a deeply loving, patient and engaged parent.

Mark yearned to be able to live up to this memory of his father in his own role as a parent to his two daughters. Unlike his parents' loving and mutually supportive relationship, however, Mark's relationship with his wife, Mandy, was fractious and difficult. Both he and Mandy worked full-time outside the home in order to make ends meet, and both were exhausted at the end of their working days, with barely enough energy to muster for themselves, let alone their children and each other.

Mark was constantly racked with guilt by the fact that he came home every night too tired and dispirited to play with his children. He hated walking into his unwelcoming, sullen and unhappy home.

Eventually, after one evening of snapping at his daughters once too often, Mark broke down into uncontrollable weeping. Mandy was so shocked by the rawness of his pain that, after years of bickering and resentment, she suddenly glimpsed once again the man that she had loved and married.

Mark and Mandy sat down and talked for many hours that night, both revealing the full depth of their respective pain and unhappiness. By the time they went to bed they had begun to work on ways to heal their lives: selling their house, reducing their working hours, going on holiday with the girls.

The point of Mark's story is that he never forgot the wonderful power of his father's and mother's unconditional love, and it was, indeed, the power of the memory of that love that saved and healed his own relationship with his wife and children. The best that we can do for our children is to try, in every moment, to express to them the unconditional love that is the very essence of our soul being.

To Recap: A Few Reminders With Which to Close

Soul and Ego in the Game of Life

At the deep centre of each of us lies our soul, the unconditionally loving essence of who we truly are. Our soul is an individual expression of the loving creative life force, the source, God, spirit, chi, prana, the Is, call it what you will, that animates the universe and everything within it.

The soul is our divine centre, the source of our capacity for love and wisdom, compassion, patience, trust and acceptance, and it learns about life and expresses itself through the tools of our ego-mind and body and through their choices and experiences in the world.

The more we make the conscious choice to live from the unconditionally loving place of soul, the more we create lives that are peaceful, useful, compassionate, loving and healing to ourselves and to everyone around us, not least – indeed most of all – to our children, who are the future of the world in the making.

The more that we practise living from soul, the more adept we become at realigning ourselves should we slip into operating purely from the ego-mind. Ego-mind actions tend to be characterised by fear, which engenders such responses to life as greed, anger, bitterness, the need to control others or indeed to try to control life, and selfishness.

It is very easy to tell when we are operating from soul. Soulful responses to life, from the language that we use to the nature of our actions, are characterised by gentleness, generosity, honesty, selflessness and a total absence of fear. They have a quality of serenity, compassion, trust, patience, acceptance and wisdom about them; above all, they are unconditionally loving. When we live from soul, we understand the interconnectedness, the oneness, of all things; to seek self-advantage over others is to seek to harm ourselves.

The Getting of Wisdom

As we acclimatise to living from our still soul centre, we become aware of the fact that our soul will always seek to deepen our compassion, our wisdom, our capacity for loving unconditionally, and our willingness to trust. Our ego-mind, comfortable with its habitual, usually fearful responses to the world, has a tendency to try to resist these 'pushes'. Our soul, however, knows when we are ready to drop down deeper into the true essence of our being. We can argue, and complain, and resist with our ego, our thoughts and our emotions, but whatever needs to arrive in our life to enable our growth will do so, and it will keep arriving until we surrender our fear and embrace our challenges fully. It can feel, sometimes, as if life is taking us in an utterly wrong direction, but when we abandon fear and meet the difficulties that we face with the innate wisdom of soul energy, we surmount those difficulties and they cease to be. Always. To sense what it feels like to operate from soul, all we have to do is simply stop, breathe deeply, contemplate the issue in hand and feel the innate wisdom that will arise, without fail, from the deepest part of our being.

The constant message of our soul is to let go of fear. There is nothing in our human lives, between the wonder of our birth and our dying, that we cannot face. Moments of ecstasy and moments of pain are all just that: moments, and they will pass. When we drop down into our soul, however, we experience the eternal, unconditionally loving creative life force of which we are an expression. That 'divine' force does not pass. It simply is, and when we truly experience it all fear ceases and we see the game of life for what it is: a game to learn from and, above all, to enjoy.

Our soul teaches us through presenting us with choices, including the choice to 'stick' or move forward. Our choice to move forward can often bring with it feelings of loss, anxiety and grieving, as certain people and circumstances in our lives fall away naturally. We can even temporarily lose our sense of meaning in life. These feelings, however deep and difficult they might be, are assuring us, however, that we are indeed moving forward: that a particular phase has come to an end. Through such changes, our soul is teaching us to trust, to love unconditionally and to let go, knowing that we will always be safe and that new people and circumstances, ones that more truly mirror who we are becoming, will appear. Our soul is always urging us to let go of attachment so that the new can enter.

The Liberation of Learning that We Are Not Our Emotions

When we are still unaware of what it is like to live from the quiet, unconditionally loving, peaceful clarity of soul, we can make the mistake of believing that we are our feelings: that our emotions are the most alive part of us, because they are the most passionate, exhilarating and exhausting expressions of ourselves. Our emotions can be provoked by many stimuli: the reaction of our senses to the physical world; our internal reactions to memory, whether conscious, unconscious or subconscious; our spontaneous responses to the actions of the people with whom we interact.

We are, however, definitely not our feelings! Strong emotional responses are nothing more than tools, guides, used by our soul wisdom to point our attention at a habit of being within ourselves (usually fear) that needs to be addressed, transformed and/or released. The key to the successful completion of this process is simply to have the courage, the soul sense, to keep our emotional hearts open: to allow ourselves to feel and explore all of our feelings, without repression, so that we can understand them for what they are (temporary and not who we are) and release them. The natural flow of our lives can be impeded by repressed feelings, which will simply tend to build up and demand expression, often as intense anger and pain. If we allow our hearts to stay open, however, we allow our feelings release so that our hearts can become free and expansive; so that they can be informed by the unconditionally loving soul nature that we truly are. Whatever life presents to us then, we can meet head on. We can allow our minds to see new possibilities, new ways to transform any current limiting situation. Hopefully, we all know people who live like this. Look at them, ask them, listen to them, and you can learn to be truly yourself.

When we do not live from soul, we tend to be absorbed by, to see only our own thoughts, our own feelings and our own place in the world. We are egocentric, even solipsistic, and tend to be lost in the past or in the future, without inhabiting the present. We see, in fact, only a small portion of what is in front of us. We are not aware of what others are thinking and feeling; we become aware only when their behaviour starts to disturb us. If we are unaware in this way, we are asleep to our true selves and to life. Only when we practise living from the still centre of our real soul being can we connect with the authentic power that we are; can we begin to see the true nature of the people and world around us; can we begin to become truly compassionate, truly wise and, above all, truly useful.

Intention and Service

From the moment that we choose to heed the calling of our deepest self and begin to drop down into that self to learn, experience and express the wonder of who we truly are, a profound and different impetus will come into our lives. As we express the intention to live from soul, and as we practise living unconditionally loving, compassionate, accepting and joyful soulful lives that grow ever deeper in wisdom and trust and move ever further away from the fear habits of our ego-mind, we become truly able to be of selfless service to the world.

In choosing to explore this book, you have already expressed the intention to discover and live from your true soul self. As you embark on this path (of which the reading of this book is but one first small step), you will begin to feel a transforming passionate enthusiasm for life, a growing love for yourself and for everyone and everything around you; you will be beginning, of course, to sense the interconnectedness, the oneness, of all things.

The practical expression of your intention will come in the soul qualities of unconditional love, patience, compassion, acceptance and trust that will increasingly come to characterise your relationship to the world around you. You will express them in your interactions with everyone you meet: friends, parents, lovers, colleagues, children, staff in the local supermarket, strangers in the street. Your growing love, compassion, wisdom and gentleness will extend themselves, too, to your relationship with the natural world around you: to the animals and plants, to the land and sea. You will become overawed by the beauty of the natural world and will want only to nurture and preserve it. Instead of reacting to life, you will become a conscious participator in life's creative process. You will become a wise instrument guided by the innate loving wisdom of your soul self, and will no longer be a reactive, fearful object, confined to what anyone might tell you that you are or are not capable of doing.

Each of us has our own unique path of soul learning and our own unique way of being of service to the world. We can each discover our true talents and let them guide us. There are no 'mistakes', only learning and opportunities. Life contains all the abundance, all the resources that we could possibly need in order to be, to express and to serve with our true soul selves. We are each unique, abundant expressions of the infinitely abundant and loving creative force that informs and animates everything that exists. There is no lack. Abundance has nothing to do with quantity. How can love, compassion, patience, acceptance, trust and wisdom be quantified? When we choose service because it is a pure expression of our unconditionally loving true selves, everything that we give will be returned to us by life, by the service of others. This is one of the essential laws of the creative loving force that is life.

What is the secret of true service? We truly serve when we develop our soul qualities to their deepest, fullest level. In doing so, we achieve the full potential of our soul, and it will inform and shine through everything that we do. In this way, we serve. We grow from being selfish to achieving selfhood, and from here we can become selfless. Exploring our true soul nature is the very beginning of this incredible, exciting, life-long process. Good luck!